SIMPIN'
AIN'T EASY

TWELVE STEPS TO EMBRACING COMMON SENSE AND

REJECTING STUPIDITY

(a memoir)

VINCENT GERVASI

ISBN: 979-8-9886310-1-9 paperback

ISBN: 979-8-89109-253-2 - ebook

Author Name: VINCENT GERVASI

Book Title: Simpin' Ain't Easy

Book Subtitle: Twelve Steps to Embracing Common Sense and Rejecting Stupidity

This book is dedicated to . . .

My mother, father, and sister. I am what I am because of our experiences.

Those who have been manipulated, lied to, and involved in toxic relationships. It is possible to free yourself from the narcissistic chains. Take ownership; you'll find your way out.

This book is also dedicated to the ones suffering from addiction inside and outside of the hallowed rooms of twelve-step programs all over the world.

Ignorance is the absence of knowledge. Stupidity is the refusal to acquire or accept it.

— KARL POPPER

TABLE OF CONTENTS

Preface. vii

Introduction ix

Chapter 1: Addiction 1

Chapter 2: Can I Bum a Smoke Off You? 11

Chapter 3: You Want to Fuck? 17

Chapter 4: Sex and Relationships 29

Chapter 5: Growth and a Different Perspective 45

Chapter 6: Victimhood vs. Happiness 57

Chapter 7: Finances and Work 71

Chapter 8: Simping Is Not Restricted to Men Only 79

Chapter 9: Simping in General 85

Chapter 10: Balancing My Life Out 91

Chapter 11: Sins of a Father 99

Chapter 12: A Boy and His Dog 105

Chapter 13: A Heartbeat Away from Oblivion. 115

Chapter 14: My Experience, Strength, and Hope. 125

Chapter 15: Conclusion 141

Bonus Chapter: Technology Is a Wonderful Thing? 145

Acknowledgments 177

Preface

I began writing this book as part of my fourth step for both my Adult Children of Alcoholics and Al-Anon NFG groups. The fourth step, as it is written in twelve-step recovery programs, states the following:

> Made a searching and fearless moral inventory of ourselves.

I have written many fourth steps over the years, and every one has been the same. For a person who has struggled with low self-worth his entire life, it was easy to list my short-comings. Self-loathing and self-deprecation come naturally to a man who, at the very minimum, doesn't like himself. This fourth step had to be different. I had to focus on the positive attributes. This was extremely difficult; I was never able to speak to my positive attributes, and if I did try to celebrate my accomplishments as a child, I was immediately chastised as a braggart or show-off. I learned that celebrating accom-plishments was not acceptable.

In this fourth step, I had to discover what my positive attributes were. This fourth step needed to be different. I needed to look for the reasons my life is important; I needed to escape the nihilistic feelings that had haunted me my entire life. I also needed to get to the root of where all these inner feelings began. Finally, I needed to discover how many of the survival traits I developed at a young age no longer serve me.

After my divorce in 2018, I was a stranger in a strange land. My ex-wife, who grew up here in the Sacramento area, moved back to San Diego. So here I am, a Southern California–grown boy in Northern California with no family, friends, or support group. Left to my best thinking, this book will outline some of the adventures that led to where I am now, some of the poor choices I made and what I needed to do to change my thinking. I will share my experience, strength, and hope and attempt to carry the message to help those who are still afflicted.

Additionally, these are my opinions and are not the opinions of any twelve-step organizations mentioned in this book. Alcoholics Anonymous, Al-Anon NFG, Adult Children of Alcoholics, and any other twelve-step programs do not support or endorse anything in this book. These are my opinions and my opinions alone.

Introduction

One of my life goals was to be able to publish my memoirs. To say I published a book would be a feather in my hat. I believe that we've all considered writing a memoir at some point in life. Well, I'm not any more special than the next person. I'm just putting down my thoughts regarding my life experiences.

A lot of what is in the following pages are some of the shittiest moments in my life—periods where my decision-making had really sunk me into deep holes physically, psychologically, and emotionally. I've also included details about the work I had to do to dig myself out of those holes.

The thirty years I'll recall were spent in and out of an alcoholic cloud. So the memories may not be completely accurate. Another thing to consider is that this is a one-sided story. I didn't interview or reach out to anyone to get their side of the story. Honestly, I don't care about their side. You could say I am being selfish. Well, yes. It's my book, and it's my perspective and my experience. What I would say to anyone who disagrees with the contents of this book is this: I challenge you to write your own book recounting the stories illustrated in this masterpiece if you feel the need for a rebuttal.

There are no conventions in this book; I'm going on strictly memory. I'll be bouncing around from the early years in my late teens to now at fifty-plus years of age. Sometimes, when expressing your ideas, you must look at the past to solve current issues. I will reference and misquote everything in this book; I'm not looking to be chronologically accurate on who said and did what. However, I will attempt to express the meaning I received from people smarter than me on the various subjects I've written on. In addition, I'll be speaking in generalities based on my experiences over the last thirty years. With that understanding, don't take anything written as a personal attack on you. However, if something that is said stings, you might consider looking in the mirror and sorting out your feelings with a therapist.

From time to time, I'll break the fourth wall. I may inject a thought or two as I'm writing in real time, well as real-time as it can get as I'm writing. I'll encapsulate random thoughts in parentheses. There will be no political correctness; at times, I'll be sarcastic (although sarcasm rarely translates well in text) and vulgar, but never crass. Much of what is in these pages I've mulled over for thirty years, sometimes revisiting situations to gain a new perspective on current events.

So what qualifies me to write a book on *simping*? Well, life experience, the ability to think, and literacy qualify me to write a book. These are my experiences. You can agree, disagree, or use the sheets in this book as toilet paper; it doesn't matter. These are my experiences and how I've interpreted life to get me here today, writing this book. I'll try to keep things in chronological order; however, as stated in the previous paragraph, in dealing with issues today, I may have to revert back to prior experiences to see if there is a lesson learned.

I'm not going to go out of my way to throw anyone under the bus. I won't explicitly out any of the people I've been in relationships with. So when discussing romantic involvement, I will just refer to them as Girlfriend #X. They can keep their anonymity, and I can avoid a lawsuit—unless they want to out themselves. However, just a reminder: court records are public.

I'll definitely be dropping names and/or shout-outs. Shout-outs may also include public figures who have done some stupid shit. Furthermore, if you have been or provided a thoughtful perspective and/or influence, you will be noted as such by name. These individuals may be personal friends or internet influencers who have given me a different perspective on life. As mentioned earlier, I'll most likely misquote the shit out of them; by no means do I mean any disrespect. I'm just too fuckin' lazy to cite everyone in this book. However, I will provide a list at the back of the book so you can research it yourself. Maybe you can pull some pearls of wisdom from their teachings.

Almost every influencer I've watched or read has said this statement in one way or another:

> Life fucking sucks; it's how you respond to it that
> separates you from the rest of humanity.

What does this mean? Well, I've interpreted it as this: Humans are miserable creatures. In general, we always look to complain about something. I'm no different; many of the people who are closest to me have heard me utter the words, "If I'm not bitchin' about something, then there is something wrong!"

There is so much to unpack in that last statement. The short version is, for most of my youth till about my mid-thirties, I was a miserable human being. Most of all, it was self-inflicted. In my later years, when my old behaviors began to creep back in, I had to take stock and revisit some old teachings learned twenty years prior. You really have to work hard to change your stripes. It isn't easy to untangle your misery and try to be a good human being. It's even harder to be virtuous—and not a simp.

So why did I title this book *Simpin' Ain't Easy* (SMPN8EZ)? I think it is first important to define the word simp:

Merriam-Webster defines *simp* as follows:

> a foolish or stupid person: SIMPLETON.

> . . . *Forrest Gump*, the smash movie starring Tom Hanks, as a sweet simp from Alabama who rides to fame and fortune on an IQ of 75.
>
> —Peter Travers

> The . . . line inching up the bottom of the chart shows the pitiful returns for the simps whose investments are taxed every year.
>
> —Virginia Wilson

> It has always been difficult to grasp how Louise, a simp in the first two-thirds of the show, could become such a swan in the final act.
>
> —Hilton Als

Urban Dictionary defines a *simp* as follows:

> A word that everyone overuses w/out the correct definition. It means a guy that is overly desperate for women, especially if she is a bad person or has expressed her disinterest in him, whom he continues to obsess over. They're usually just virgins that will accept coochie (aka, pussy) from anyone regardless of who they are.

This is how I define simp as it pertains to my own life experiences:

> Investing time, money, emotional and physical energy for little to no return on investment (ROI).

Now that we all have a clear understanding of the definition, we can see where I have bounced in and out of these different forms of "simpness," choosing the wrong people or just plain being ignorant. In this context, I will lay out some of the bad choices I've made in my life and the consequences that followed in pursuit of affection, attention, and affirmation. Maybe I can illustrate how I've twelve-stepped my way out of these scenarios. So sit back and enjoy the ride.

Chapter 1
Addiction

Merriam-*Webster* defines *addiction* as "a compulsive, chronic, physiological, or psychological need for a habit-forming substance, behavior, or activity having harmful physical, psychological, or social effects and typically causing well-defined symptoms (such as anxiety, irritability, tremors, or nausea) upon withdrawal or abstinence."

I cannot begin writing on a topic so real to so many individuals without relaying my addictions. I firmly believe that most people suffer from one addiction or another. Addictions take many forms, as expressed in the definition above. I also believe that most people practice their addictions without knowing they are addicted. I am also of the opinion that once aware of their addictions, they gladly choose to ignore them because the alternative would mean looking in the mirror and changing their behavior. In most circumstances, people are afraid to change, including the author of this book. It takes an enormous amount of courage to face the demons inside, where all demons live.

As mentioned earlier, I have my own addictions; for dramatic effect, I will refer to my addictions as demons. My demons include alcohol, nicotine, and in my life, the most seductive of demons: women. I will embark on a journey in my mind and hopefully provide you, the reader, with some pearls of wisdom I've picked up over my short fifty years on this earth. By opening up, maybe, I can learn a little more about myself and entertain you while on this journey.

I realized early on, at seventeen, that alcohol was a potent elixir. It gave me superhuman powers of the mind. Alcohol allowed a very insecure individual to come out of his shell and be the life of the party, the hero of the day, and the ultimate lover and unleashed an intelligence that was superior and could rival any of today's top minds. Just ask me about it. I would love to pontificate on it.

I realized very quickly that it was all a con job, and fortunately for me, at a very young age, I realized it was all my own mental masturbation. Stroking my very sensitive ego until it all came crashing down after my second DUI (driving under the influence).

Lying on my mother's couch after a second night in jail within an eighteen-month period, I realized my life had to change—drastically. However, I had no idea how this would take place. In forty-five days, I had to appear in court and hand my life over to the People's Court of Los Angeles and a judge who most likely wouldn't be lenient.

Forty-five days later, once the sentence was passed, I did what any young, inexperienced knucklehead would do: I went home to ask my mother for help. I needed someone outside of myself to bail me out of the dumb-ass decision I had made—driving drunk. Think about that for a minute; as an adult, I had to ask Mommy to bail me out.

The courts had other stipulations in mind in lieu of court fines. In addition, the Department of Motor Vehicles suspended my driver's license for eighteen months. I was also sentenced to an alcohol diversion program and eighteen months of Alcoholics Anonymous meetings. I participated in AA for sixty months, identifying as an alcoholic.

During those years, I learned many valuable lessons. First and foremost, don't drink and drive. And a further deep dive into my life via the twelve-step program (AA), there was an underlying message I still haven't forgotten.

Wait for it . . .

RESPONSIBILITY!

The root word for *responsibility*, as defined by *Merriam-Webster*, is *responsible*: "liable to be called on to answer."

Now let's take a minute to define *liable*, again as defined by *Merriam-Webster*: "obligated according to law or equity."

Obligated to law? Whose law? Man's law? God's law? Mother Nature's law? Then tack on the second part of the definition, "or equity." What the fuck does that mean? Well, let's refer to **Merriam-Webster** again:

> Equity: Justice according to natural law or right specifically: freedom from bias or favoritism.

Going down this rabbit hole isn't getting any clearer; it raises more questions than answers. Equitable to whom? The answer may be in the definition of "according to natural law":

> Natural law is a philosophical and legal concept that refers to a system of principles or rules that are inherent in the natural world and govern human behavior. These principles are believed to be discoverable through reason and observation, rather than being dependent on human invention or social convention.
>
> In other words, natural law posits that there are certain fundamental ethical principles that are objectively true and universally applicable, regardless of cultural or historical context. These principles are often seen as being derived from nature, the cosmos, or a divine source, and are thought to provide a basis for moral and legal judgments.

Examples of natural law principles include the right to life, liberty, and property; the duty to fulfill promises; and the prohibition against harming others without just cause. These principles are often contrasted with positive law, which refers to man-made laws that are created by governments or other legal authorities.

Keep these words in mind as we progress through this book. Also, this definition doesn't sound like anything the leftists are yelling about. Things that make you go, hmm!

Let's return to the young man in his early twenties lying on his mother's couch, realizing that life can't be this fucked up. I was constantly looking for others to bail me out of my own bad decisions, seeking substances to cure me of my shortcomings. More about shortcomings later, alcohol provided me with the ability to be something other than I am. Alcohol also provided me with an excuse for the lack of direction in my life and allowed me to blame everything on everyone else.

This is the seduction. It is difficult to sort through people's minds, much less my own, in a diluted alcoholic fog. Anyone who says they have a lock on life, I say great! However, if I've learned anything from playing poker, it is that everyone is a bullshitter, even when they are not bullshitting. Everything is a setup.

For the sake of getting through this chapter, I'll begin with, "It's all my parents' fault," and they are the ones who fucked me up (more on this in a minute).

do not have children, so I cannot write about the complexties of child-rearing. However, we all have had some adults n our lives trying to teach us about growing up. All that being said, some people do it better than others. I grew up in the burbs, the most eastern part of Los Angeles County, my parents were immigrants to the United States, and I had a lower-middle-class upbringing. Not a horrible existence. My parents did the best they could with what they had, bringing to the table their own set of biases and baggage. I am not criticizing them; I truly believe they wanted what was best for me, much like most parents. Since raising children does not come with a manual, I believe they imparted me with the gift of thinking differently. I sure as hell wasn't going to think the way they did.

At this point, I want to take a break and allow you, the reader, to jump ship. This rabbit hole will run deep and raise many questions in your mind, some dark places that may be too scary to travel. You can stop reading here if you'd like. (You have my permission to use the remaining pages as toilet paper unless you're reading this digitally; it's not advised that you flush your electronic device down the toilet.) For the brave and interested, I invite you to grab your favorite addiction (alcohol, herbal remedies, soft drink, food, caffeine, etc.) and travel with me through my mind.

It was June 18, 1994. (If that date sounds vaguely familiar, we were all captivated by the O. J. Simpson car chase on the news the night before, June 17, 1994.) I was twenty-two, and it was the morning after I was released from jail, lying on my mother's couch, full of shame, guilt, and despair. In a nutshell I was feeling like a complete loser, much like a champion racehorse tripping over its own legs out of the starting gate. I had lost my driver's license and would soon lose my job as a result. On June 17, the night before, I was barhopping with friends and pulled over for making an illegal U-turn arrested, incarcerated, and soon to be convicted of a second DUI. (Coincidently, I was driving a white Ford SUV.)

A year earlier, I had finished my associate degree in electronics from one of those tech schools advertised on television. I was a field service representative traveling and repairing equipment throughout the United States. I traveled to and from many of the States on the continent and brought down a decent salary for a twenty-two-year-old. In one night of celebrating and indulging in my own arrogance, it was all taken away just like that. In addition, I had my sights on going to Warrant Officer Candidate School and becoming a helicopter pilot in the United States Army Reserves. All those dreams were shot to hell because of one night of drinking.

Much like the narrator in *Fight Club*, the next ten years were spent in twelve-step programs trying to figure out how fucked up I am, debating philosophy and psychology and attempting to get a handle on my life, completely oblivious to the answers in front of me. The addiction was real, and I know many people can relate. In fact, just recently, I read a meme on Instagram:

> Is this what life is about, trading one addiction for another?

So many of us have an inability to live with ourselves without external stimulation. Combined with my nicotine addiction, overeating, and love for women, I was a ticking time bomb, never really getting a hold of what life was about.

Abstaining from booze for five years did teach me that I, as a human being, am capable of doing whatever I want. Sound familiar, "You can be anything you want, even the president of the United States"? What is missing from that statement is "... if you are willing to accept the responsibility that comes with it."

I am the last person on this planet to pass judgment on anyone. (I won't be casting the first stone, maybe the second or third—human nature.) What I will say is if you choose a lifestyle that requires you to compromise yourself and your integrity as a human being and put yourself or others in harm's way, you need to accept your responsibility in those transactions. Examples of this don't have to be dramatic; they can be as subtle as a dispute regarding property lines among neighbors.

We, as humans, are inherently selfish creatures. We come out of the womb as such; we are ego driven and will always strive to take care of our own needs selfishly and, most of the time, at the expense of others. You don't have to look far; look at the teenagers we are raising today.

This is what addiction is to me; this is how I define my addiction—deep compulsive needs to fill a hole in my psyche, an external want for sedation that can only be satiated by an internal wholeness. Wow! That was a brief moment of stoner enlightenment; I digress.

Blaming my parents for fucking my life up, I gave myself an out for many years. I didn't take responsibility for myself because I am the fruit of their loins. The fruit doesn't fall from the tree. They are the people at fault, not me. I am a product of my environment. Sound familiar?

The wonderful thing about blaming your environment, people, places, and things is that it allows you to avoid any responsibility until responsibility catches up with you. After you've alienated everyone in your life, after you've been alienated, the only person you have left is you. Now what?

I have a drinking problem (substitute drinking with overeating, gambling, sex/porn, social media, drugs, shopping, debt, nicotine, whatever). Addictions consume you slowly; life begins to have no meaning. You become more nihilistic, more narcissistic, and more self-loathing. Later, I discovered that it wasn't my drinking; it was my thinking. (We'll touch on that concept later.)

The more I partook in my addictions, the deeper that hole in the pit of my stomach got. I couldn't control or, at a minimum, satiate the compulsion.

It took five years, but I managed to get my driver's license back, pay back all the fines, return to school, and earn my undergraduate degree. At a tremendous cost, I had to learn my first lesson in responsibility, sometimes working two jobs to settle my court fines and pay astronomical insurance fees, all while trying to pay my way through school. The end result was good, for the most part. However, life took on a different trajectory based on some really bad decisions. Choices you make today affect future choices (or lack of choices). Those damn DUIs still pop up on live scans even today, regardless of the thirty years that separate me from them.

Chapter 2
Can I Bum a Smoke Off You?

I've had an on-and-off love affair with nicotine, and still to this day, as I am writing this book, I don't understand my need to kill myself. The studies are out; we all know the ill effects of smoking. Maybe through writing this, I may discover an answer. At the moment, my thought process is, if I do not find a solution in my own heart and mind regarding this toxic relationship with nicotine—like my grandparents and extended family that have passed on—smoking can and will be my demise.

I have no one else to blame other than myself. My love affair with nicotine started around the same time I discovered alcohol, around high school, to be a part of a group and be included. High school sucks, though I know some people may disagree. In my life, though, it was hard; I never belonged to any one clique. I played sports, hung out with the Hessians (metal heads as defined by the period in the '80s), thoroughly enjoyed home economics class, and hung out with members of the high school band.

I was all over the board when it came to my social circles. Everyone had their own way of being, and everyone was trying to figure out what the fuck was going on. I was no different. Regardless of the fact that I was socializing with

11

different groups, I never felt like I fit in entirely. I'll tell you what, though, smoking and drinking helped smooth things over.

I do remember a significant rivalry between the water polo team and the football players, of which I was a part. Yes, I played football. I was a proud member of the third string, too small and too slow to make the first string but crazy enough to be on special teams, affectionately known as the Suicide Squad. The amount of testosterone at that age was insane. (By the way, testosterone isn't a bad thing.) I have to reference Dr. Jordan B. Peterson at this point:

> You should be a monster. An absolute monster. And then you should learn to control it.

> This is what learning to live with testosterone means. In every young man, the monster should be cultivated, and furthermore, a young man needs to control it. This is how nature intended; after all, we are animals, animals with consciousness.

We all want to be a part of something; I stopped smoking for the better part of six years until I met a woman who was a smoker. I fell fast and hard. She was everything I wanted in a woman; she was beautiful, funny, intelligent, witty, and sarcastic. When we first met, I chose to engage in my addiction to nicotine for much the same reasons I fell into smoking when I was in high school. I wanted to be part of something, to be accepted, even though it meant compromising my health, one cigarette at a time, until I am now smoking two to three packs a week.

I want you to pay close attention to some of my verbiage. Earlier, I said "chose" because I made a conscious decision to smoke instead of "fell" as if there was no choice and avoiding responsibility like it was some accident. There is a distinction here; the former "chose" implies I am taking responsibility. The latter implies no fault of my own. This is significant because my ego does not want to be accountable. It hurts too much to admit to myself that I am the cause of my own self-harm. Our minds will justify anything if we leave them unchecked.

I guess this is what high school and college are all about, learning to socialize and being part of a community. However, since the pandemic, it seems that it has gotten much more complicated for young people. In many ways, I am grateful there was limited access to technology when I was in school. I barely navigated social situations in the wild. I can't imagine having to handle social situations hiding behind technology and all of its consequences.

Getting back to high school, it was hard enough to find social circles you fit into. I can't imagine having gender-bending ideology mixed into the equation to really fuck your shit up. However, most of the students at that time, if they hadn't come out of the closet, most of us knew or understood. There was really no conversation regarding sexuality or gender. However, I believe my generation was much more accepting than previous generations. I believe this is true even today. However, it seems like the conversation is strictly limited to one side.

During my college years, I questioned my sexual preference for a brief time. I couldn't understand why my relationships with men were far more straightforward than my relationships with women. I found out that I do love the vagina (the greatest thing since sliced bread). Secondly, a hairy asshole does not titillate me. I sought out the consultation of a friend who is gay and a good human being. I had an open conversation regarding my dilemma. He explained that it was perfectly natural to question who I was at my age. However, he gave me two pieces of evidence to show I wasn't gay:

1. I wasn't born gay. Questioning my sexuality never came up in my early years until a bad breakup with a woman in my early twenties.

2. I kept getting involved with toxic women.

He continued to explain my experiences with women have been with less-than-desirable human beings. It was only natural to question the health and quality of these relationships. I didn't realize it then, but this was the beginning of my simping career (hence the title of this book).

In my mid-twenties, a new concept was introduced called *political correctness*. At the time, I wasn't clear on what it truly meant. To be completely transparent, I didn't know that political correctness started from old Stalinist and Maoist concepts in the '50s and '60s. Essentially it was a leftist technique to control speech.

How does this tie into simping? This is the introduction to buying into a concept that doesn't make sense or contradicts what your fundamental ideas are—watching what one says in fear that you will offend someone. Slowly, over the years, modern-day feminism has taken root in our culture. So wanting to get laid, I naturally subscribed to the concept of,

"You go, girl, you're stunning and brave," sexual liberation, burn the bra and whatnot!

Being a kind and sweet friend and an ear to listen, as well as assuring my target relationship, I was a different kind of man. I conceded to the whims of women until I was unrecognizable to myself. This is the worst kind of man: a coward. The simp is the cunning snake in the grass waiting for the right moment, as he is patient and manipulative. I disgust myself thinking about how low I would go to get laid—and avoid the responsibility of being a productive, virtuous man in society.

I pretended to be the hero (to cover up the fact that I was a coward). Alcohol helped; it made me into everything I didn't have the character for. Even though I was getting laid over the years, the simping in relationships caused me to lose my net gains in life. Let me use different phrasing; the juice wasn't worth the squeeze. I invested too much time, energy, and money into the wrong people. The most catastrophic result was that I compromised myself. The work to find my integrity and build it back was that much more difficult once compromised. It is much easier to put in the work earlier in life than taking shortcuts and trying to undo the wreckage later.

However, being a simp isn't all one-sided; women who recognize a simp will take advantage and use his simpleness against him. She'll ask you to watch her kids while she goes to work at the strip joint. She'll call you to wire her money at all hours of the night so she can get her next high and bang her drug dealer. She will use her vagina against you and withhold pussy if you get out of line.

As a simp, your lack of self-respect will make you do almost anything to avoid abandonment. For example, buying her old house so she can move into her new house, what a paradox. I fear abandonment, yet she purchased a new home to move away from me. WTF? Where in fuck's sake is that fucking logical? Pussy, when not put in the correct perspective, will make simps do stupid shit. Believe me, I did some stupid shit.

Chapter 3

You Want to Fuck?

In my mid-twenties, I bartended my way through my undergrad degree at the same school I mentioned earlier, the one advertised on TV. I had a different outlook regarding alcohol because of my relationship with Bill W. (Google it). I really enjoyed this time in my life, specifically, my ego: "Being a bartender is a power trip. I am the show, I am here to entertain you, I am here to serve you your favorite elixir, and I am here to get laid. In fact, I enjoyed it so much that I didn't have the energy to bring women home at the end of my drink-slinging days. I burnt out hard and fast. However, it didn't quell the addiction for women.

I've said this time and time again: women are the greatest invention since sliced bread. You can quote me on it. There is nothing more dangerous, cunning, manipulative, demoralizing, beautiful, exotic, enticing, exciting, and loving than a woman. If you're gay, well, to quote Katt Williams, "This ain't your part of the show!" (I'll get to my opinions regarding the LGBTQ+ community in a later chapter). Where I'm going with this, regardless of what your experience is, to propagate the species, we need both sexes. I refuse to give my opinions regarding sexual orientation at this point in the book. Plus, I've already touched on some of my experiences earlier.

Back to the story, with my bartending background out there, my longtime friend Tim and I liked to frequent bars, much like many twenty-somethings like to do today. We frequented a club in Huntington Beach, California (Gecko's), which has long been replaced by a family-style Italian restaurant.

Before Gecko's being bulldozed, Sunday nights were the best. It was hard rock night. A Long Beach radio station (KNAC) sponsored the night, providing local radio person-alities and heavy metal music—everything from Anthrax to White Zombie. I loved this scene. It was the night when all the hooligans came out in their Sunday best leather, dog collars, chains, metal studs, and spikes (like the Blue Oyster Bar without all the gayness).

As we cleared the doorman and walked into the club, Tim and I eyed a very attractive five-foot-four blonde, with a slender build, wearing a white leather cocktail dress and five-inch heels to match her dress. At that exact moment, my friend leaned in my direction and, under his breath, but loud enough I could hear over the music, said, "Wanna fuck?" simultane-ously pointing toward the hot blonde. She quickly eyed my friend and responded, "No thank you." At that point, I lost it; I damn near fell on my ass laughing. It was classic.

I wish relationships were that easy; they aren't. Imagine a world where we didn't have to pretend, where it was as easy as asking a question, "Wanna fuck?" and getting a simple acceptable response, either, "No, thank you!" or "Yes, please," and all parties involved not getting their egos bruised or offended.

Some more anecdotal evidence, again, I was bartending, and there was a particular brunette that caught my eye. We were flirting and having fun throughout the evening, nothing outside the ordinary. She returned to the bar and was concerned about a male patron making her and her friends uncomfortable. Thinking on my feet, I told her I knew how to get rid of him. She had a curious look on her face. I asked her to open her mouth wide, and I sprayed whipped cream into her mouth and planted a big wet kiss on her. We dated for about six months after that kiss. And needless to say, her stalker left her and her friends alone that night.

Feminism is fickle; if you aren't Chad Thundercoque, you'll be labeled a creep. However, the good-looking bartender can shove his tongue down her throat and everything is fine, everything is peaches and sunshine. That last story really didn't need to be told; it was an ego booster, me living out my Al Bundy glory days. (Google it.) It was also to draw out the hypocrisy that the feminist movement has generated. What is significant is that men, just like women, want to be wanted. Hypergamy aside, it is in our nature to partner up. But what happens when perspectives shift, societal pressures take root, and my dick stops working?

We've all heard the cliche that youth is wasted on the young. What the fuck does that mean? I had a great time making good and bad decisions in my youth, and I still make good and bad decisions today. We are human; we are fallible—I'll be making my point shortly. Regardless of the decisions I've made, life still goes on. Young or old, life keeps moving. Unfortunately, I can't say that I have no regrets. I try to keep my regrets to a minimum, and I try to learn from all my adventures. The most extraordinary adventures have always revolved around women. Mind you, I did not say conquests or notches on the belt; I said adventures. There are many euphemisms here, but I'll try to keep it above a junior high level.

Since I brought it up, let's talk about my dick (penis). I've gone to physicians, and my testosterone levels are good. I am still horny as I ever was in high school, and I still find sex pleasurable . . . for the most part. However, in the most recent years, there has been a fundamental shift in my perspective. Generally speaking, women aren't fun anymore.

Now, I feel that it is necessary to qualify that last statement. In general, when you get to be my age, it is expected that you have baggage, hopefully well-managed baggage, like good organization in your garage. Most people manage their lives like they manage the storage in their garage. They stuff things in any corner with no method or organization until they can't fit anything else, much less a car in their garage. As a result, when trying to locate the Baby Jesus of the nativity set, they can't find him because he's stuffed in a box with last year's dildo collection. (Yes . . . yes, I went there.)

Where I'm going with this is that most people, men and women alike, haven't sorted through the wreckage of their past, the junk in the metaphorical garage. The women I've experienced are still sorting through their body counts (Google it) and past relationships, bringing a long history of crap to the table. Because of this, ultimately, we as men end up getting compared to and suffering the consequences of shit we had nothing to do with. So I feel empathetic toward the guy who has to sort through the box labeled "Vince" in my ex's garage. I believe this is where the statement, "Men! They are all the same," comes from. The women we (men) come in contact with have not dealt with or sorted their garages (no pun intended). And, in some cases are incapable of distinguishing good men from bad.

Here is where my past catches up with me, and there is a valuable lesson to be learned. I have had several long-lasting relationships over my short life. My shortest relationship was overnight, my most extended ten years. On average, I have had relationships that have lasted five to seven years. Don't bother trying to do the math; I lost count years ago. I thoroughly enjoy being in relationships. I like sharing the mundane and playing house. Now, I use the word *mundane* because the parties involved aren't living an adventure when they are knee-deep in rent, mortgages, car payments, taking care of kids or pets, and grocery shopping. What I like about relationships is the potential to build your own little empire that can be shared between two consenting adults. Fantasy? Maybe. I do believe that relationships can be complex, however, not for the obvious reasons you may think.

Again, I don't bother doing the math regarding my body count (Google it). However, I've been in enough relationships to where I've diluted my chances of having a successful relationship if I don't take responsibility for my own expectations (or organizing my garage, so to speak).

In society, specifically Western society, roles have changed dramatically. Today we have a lot of women who have foregone the role of mother and caretaker to pursue careers and become powerful figureheads, which is a remarkable statement for Western society.

On the other side of that coin, men's role in society has significantly digressed. At one point in time, men were taught to get a job, get a car, get educated (not necessarily formally), get married, buy a home, have kids, and, if they make it long enough, retire to enjoy their grandchildren. In short, be the protector and provider. What I am seeing in men now (particularly younger men) is that they no longer possess the drive to be providers and role models. Men are being blamed for the ills in society (Toxic masculinity, WTF, is that?), no longer want to engage in a competition of any sort (unless it's in women's sports), and would rather live virtually while getting high.

Furthermore, to that extreme, men no longer want to participate in society. Essentially, men are Men Going Their Own Way (MGTOW) and do not bother with relationships or partake directly in society.

Back to my penis, as of this writing, I consider myself single. Hook-up culture has its benefits. I have all the fun without commitment, thank you, social media, dating apps, and modern-day feminism. To that end, having been married, Western culture and law are not family-friendly, much less man-friendly. There is no benefit to marriage for men; through the advent of no-fault divorce, for the most part, women get the parting prize, and men get left with debt, homelessness, childlessness, and potentially suicide. So hook-up culture is the short-term remedy; all the benefits of getting laid have little to no "upfront" costs, or so it seems.

Until #MeToo. As mentioned earlier in my previous adventure, a man of average looks and stature merely looks in the direction of a modern woman, and this simple act can land him jobless and potentially incarcerated. However, if a man is Chad Thundercoque or Tyrone Longdong, he has his pick and sorts through women as if he were sorting through his underwear drawer. Dating apps have commoditized women, and both sexes are getting hosed (in a metaphorical sense). Social media and dating apps have reduced the vagina (the greatest thing since sliced bread) to a meat holster.

In addition, social media has inflated the egos of women. Below-average women in looks and stature seek the top 5 percent of men. The Chads and Tyrones, the high-income earners, over six feet tall, six-pack abs, six-inch dick . . . you get the point. All the while, Chad and Tyrone are laughing their way through the pussy bank, getting laid with no commitment. Their bedrooms are revolving doors for new vaginas to walk through, while the underwhelming men fill up the inboxes of women who aren't particularly attractive (low-hanging fruit), inflating the egos of, well, ugly women. All the while, modern women wonder, "Where are all the good men?" The answer is simple: both corporate and educational institutions have subscribed to a woke ideology. (Put a pin in that thought. We'll get back to it.)

The simps and feminists have forced the good men to check out. The juice isn't worth the squeeze. (Where have we heard that before?) Men have always been able to provide for themselves and typically live minimalist lifestyles. So why invest time, money, and energy in a meat holster? That's right, I've reduced the vagina (the greatest thing since sliced bread) to a masturbation tool. Fortunately, men have two meat holsters built in, Ms. Left and Ms. Right. Throw in some saucy videos, and you have an instant orgy. However, jerking your tube steak impulsively is not recommended; use that energy and do something constructive.

Let's take a short walk along memory lane pre-pandemic, March of 2020. My divorce was finalized in May of 2018, and dating apps were the way to meet people, or so that's what I thought. Many of the frustrations you feel on dating apps, I didn't experience. I had little to no issue getting laid. However, most of what I was pulling out of that pond wasn't worth bringing home to Momma. Then the "one" showed up on my screen; I was instantly attracted to her dark hair and hazel eyes. I sent a message and quickly made a connection. I knew and stated in a message that she and I could make all kinds of bad decisions together—and we did.

However, lockdowns were being enforced, and our first date quickly looked like a long shot. We had agreed to meet at an Irish pub for St. Patrick's Day, but lockdowns were coming hard and fast except for essential facilities. Again, thinking on my feet, I asked, "Do you need to do some grocery shopping?" Our first date was at a grocery store. We walked down every aisle and had fun. Of course, there was alcohol involved— but not what you're thinking: she filled her cart with wine, and I filled my cart with beer. We both drove home sober.

Of course, much like many of my previous relationships, it started out hot and heavy. I'll spare the bedroom details, but it was intense. I am still turned on by her today, but the relationship was toxic as hell. I could quickly point the finger at her and spare my ego from the realization of responsibility. We could even get into all the straws that finally came together to break this camel's back. The reality is that she saved me from me. This relationship was the catalyst that opened me up to the possibility that my failures in my relationships may begin with me. Since then, I've been to many counseling groups, therapists, and life coaches in an attempt to clean and sort out my garage.

Over the years, I cannot tell you how in some cases having an outside disinterested third party can help you get through some tough times. However, some of the traditional therapies I've gone through tended to look at the inner child, rehash parental relationships, and so on. The issue for me regarding traditional therapy is I was simply tired of rehashing my relationship in regard to my parents. I know they fucked up. I know I fucked up as an adult regarding parental relations. So rehashing old wounds and mistakes did not affect my recovery. Simply put, I had dealt with family history and could no longer let my parents take the blame for my decisions as an adult. It doesn't make sense to continue to play the victim role for something that happened in the past.

It wasn't until an old classmate from high school suggested I look into his life coach that I was able to have some break-throughs. I am happy I considered his suggestion. This journey took me through my most recent relationships, with both men and women, business and personal. The counseling helped reinforce what I've always known from the early days of AA: Everything I do on this earth, good, bad, or indifferent, begins with me. I am the common denominator in all my inter-actions. And how I interact with life on life's terms is solely my responsibility.

The process was straightforward, yet the hardest thing to do—develop a relationship with myself. Much like my father, I have ridden the coattails of the women in my life. I don't need to share the dynamics of my father's life, but I will share my own. I associated my identity with the women in my life. Because I had not developed my own, I had no principal foundation to build on. Instead, I allowed the vagina to be the chasm (no pun intended) between myself and the human I wanted to be.

I subscribed to the mentality of a happy wife, happy life. I am here to tell you, without a doubt, that this concept is bullshit. I changed my life in many of my relationships to accommodate my counterpart. In doing so, I compromised myself. I sold myself out, much like Metallica did on the *Black Album*, thinking if I catered to others, I would find happiness. Instead, I found myself whining about Napster in court and how unfair the software was while losing myself and my bassist in the process (metaphorically speaking). Much like the band mentioned above, it is a long, hard road of self-analyzing, slowly bringing me back to what is in alignment.

Since the *Black Album* to now, my life has been a long hard road of self-realization.

Self-betrayal is a motherfucker. Every time I relented, every time I bent the knee, every time I conceded, I sold myself out. I betrayed myself for the insatiable appetite of my counterpart. Damn, what a dopamine hit it was when she patted me on the head and said, "Good boy." There is a pattern in all of my relationships, the self-destructive behavior, the constant seeking of validation, the horrifying realization that I am at the root of my addictions. My mistake early in life was thinking that I had to prove myself to others to feel self-worth. Paradoxically, the only person I have to prove my worth to is myself.

Social media and society at large prey on these emotions, and we seek out the dopamine hit. Everyone seeks likes, validation, approval, attention, and affirmation. Here are some questions to consider if you are struggling:

1. Do you like yourself?

2. What are your addictions?

3. How do you play a role in your own life?

4. Consider what your life would be if you created your own validations independent of your peers?

Chapter 4
Sex and Relationships

This is a topic that everyone finds taboo, which is odd because this subject is arguably at the root of all our grief as humans—the wanting of intimacy from another. I'm really not interested in what your sexual market value score (SMV) is (SMV is a reference to Rollo Tomassi); more about this later. However, I believe that most, if not all, of us want a life partner that can help lessen the burden that life serves up. In my own personal experience, I've been guilty of that, wanting someone in my life that is a partner to take over the world with or, at a minimum, build an empire of comfort.

I classify myself as a hedonist to one degree or another. Time to reference *Merriam-Webster* again. The definition of a *hedonist* is "a person who is devoted to the pursuit of pleasure."

There are many things in life you may consider pleasurable. For me, it is alcohol, nicotine, and the best pleasure, women, as discussed in the first chapter. The lengths I have put my body, soul, finances, and mental health through in the pursuit of pussy are incalculable. I won't bore you with the history of all my sexual and personal pursuits. However, I will lay out (no pun intended) the significant influences in my life. I have already mentioned my most recent relationship, and, again, I won't be throwing anyone under the bus. I'll respect the anonymity of those involved.

As mentioned in the first chapter, my most recent relationship was hard and fast (again, no pun intended). However, Girlfriend #5 was fucking hot, with exotic hazel eyes and dark hair and of Mediterranean descent. We shared many of the same pleasures: food, drink, and sex. She had two children and was widowed; this is where you, the audience, get to judge me and say, "You missed the red flags!" No, I didn't miss the red flags; I ignored them because Girlfriend #5 was different. In hindsight, no, no, she wasn't different, just a different form of crazy. However, this book isn't about Girlfriend #5; this book is about my decisions and what brought me here to this point in life, writing this book. Prior to now, I began looking for an answer to one question:

Why do I continue to attract unavailable women?

A generic question, but a pertinent one. In my experience, all my relationships began hot and heavy; the steamy cardinal-colored glasses blinded me to many things, including boundaries. Boundaries, what the fuck are those? I believe that we all attempt to put our best foot forward in new relationships; we give it all away because it's new and exciting. We share intimate details about our lives, hoping the prospect of a new relationship and the person we involve ourselves with accepts us for who we are. We verbally vomit our most intimate details because we want our potential partner to accept us. Ultimately, we share too much too soon; many of us have experienced some seriously fucked-up shit. In doing so, we begin a relationship based on shared traumas, telling one another that we are toxic because o these horrific experiences. By doing so, we can justify our future bad behavior.

The first three months of any new relationship are great until you start spending the night together and eventually move in. Then the real relationship begins to show itself. Before we move on, I need to preface this by saying that moving forward, I feel my statements will be just as factual for women as they are for men.

When the rose-colored glasses come off, everything is exposed. I won't get too far into all of the intimate details, but I will tell you that in light of everything, I attempted to love Girlfriend #5 unconditionally—which is easier said than done. It isn't in our nature to do so, to love someone unconditionally. (We can argue that point later.) To the point loving someone unconditionally is not an intelligent thing to do, it is naive to think in such terms. Love and sex are a small part of relationships. However, we as humans subscribed to the fucking fairy tales we were told as children, forgetting the fact that what we've been told is a fucking fairy tale.

In my fifty years, the one thing that has made itself crystal clear is that love is transactional. Spoiler alert, love is transactional, depending on the value of the relationship and your tolerance to deal with your partner's idiosyncrasies. Love depends solely on how much drama, bullshit, or chaos you are willing to allow in your life. Marriage, relationships, and love are all transactional. Since the dawn of human beings on this earth, love has been transactional.

Women, in general, are hypergamous in nature, meaning they are constantly on the lookout for the man that can provide them with safety and security. (These terms are used loosely.) Women have the cards stacked against them in nature, meaning they are the most vulnerable, specifically during childbirth and child-rearing. So it is in their nature that women choose wisely for a mate that can provide them safety and security. Fast-forward a few millennia and add a dash of Western culture, and, voila, safety and security come in the way of money, power, and influence. Hypergamy is still there, but in a utilitarian sense; it changed with technology and modern culture.

NOTE: In today's culture, women are only vulnerable when pregnant and in child-rearing. Western culture has put women on a pedestal, assuming they are vulnerable in all aspects of life. Women are human; they are very capable of all that is wrong with humanity, including and not limited to murder, lying, cheating, and stealing, perhaps even more heinous, manipulative, and cunning than men. (Shout-out to Hillary Clinton.)

Today, since women are making the paper (money) and rising to positions of power, they no longer require the safety and security of a man in their lives. They can afford childcare, and when children are old enough, the public school systems provide childcare. The traditional role of men has gone the way of the dodo. In the event of lower-income/single-parent homes, Big Daddy Government will be more than happy to step in to fill the financial gap.

Men, on the other hand, haven't changed much in our roles. We still operate with the mindset of providers; that's what we were designed to do. Hunt to provide food, seek shelter, and keep a fire burning to ward away dangerous animals. In the 1950s, the men went to work, and the women stayed home to take care of the home front. Dad would come home, hoping there was no drama and/or catastrophes and, least of all, headaches. To summarize, pair bonding is transactional. Love is transactional; either party has to give up something to gain something. It really boils down to that. What will you transact to feel the warmth and fuzzies inside (seeking attention, approval, and/or affection)?

Needless to say, my relationship with Girlfriend #5 was a hard one to get over. I put so much of myself into the relationship, much like previous relationships, so much so that I lost myself. Or maybe I never understood who I was? This relationship had life-altering consequences, and I visited a psychiatrist for six months after the primary breakup. It was a turbulent on-and-off, back-and-forth type of thing till January 2022. (It could also be coined the heroin relationship—she was an addiction.) I asked the question at the beginning of the chapter, for those of you that don't remember, "Why do I continue to attract unavailable women?" It's a complex answer, and it all returns to the guy in the mirror.

Remember, I said that relationships are transactional. I am the type of guy who believes you get out of something what you put into it. I'm an all-in type. I refuse to go into anything if I am not rewarded. Nor will I go into a situation if I am unwilling to put everything into it (give it the old college try). I also expect my partner to do the same—keyword "expect" (definition time). The third definition for *expect* in *Merriam-Webster* is "to consider bound in duty or obligated."

So by this definition, if I behave in a particular manner, for example, kind, loyal, generous, and loving, it is justified to *expect* the same in return. Transactional!

What happens when your partner doesn't act in kind? Then it is in our nature to doubt the relationship. You begin to doubt your choice and second-guess yourself. The relationship isn't what you thought it would be when you had those shiny new cardinal-colored glasses on.

What if the relationship explodes into violence? Let's take a moment to define *violence*. As per *Merriam-Webster*, the third definition of violence is "an intense, turbulent, or furious and often destructive action or force; the violence of the storm, a vehement feeling or expression and a clashing or jarring quality."

While the relationship with Girlfriend #5 was not physically violent, she had a way of expressing herself with vehement feelings, so much so that I had to call a disinterested third party to get her ass back in check. Yes, I called the police; being a single, middle-aged white man and having experienced many friends being put in jail, falsely accused of domestic violence, I felt at that moment I needed to get this situation under control.

Several events preceding this night foreshadowed this particular evening, but I ignored them because I wanted so badly to love Girlfriend #5 without conditions. I *chose* to ignore them. I allowed myself into that situation. It was my decision. Where it stands now, I can say that I still love Girlfriend #5. I love her from an arm's distance. I love her the way I love most of humanity. We are all ignorant humans trying to make our way in life. Today, I cannot allow myself to be in her life. This type of relationship will kill you or, at a minimum, some part of you.

We, as humans, have a way of trading our souls with the devil for those things that might bring us happiness. I am not comparing Girlfriend #5 to the devil; quite the contrary, she may have saved my life. If it weren't for my experience, I might have never learned those lessons that were required to be learned. I am a glutton for punishment, and I'll share a few more stories to prove that I love getting my ass kicked.

Before Girlfriend #5, I was married for five years, a relatively short marriage in the scope of things; however, I dated my then fiancée for three years. Before meeting Wife #1, I considered myself to be successful. In May of 2010 I closed escrow on a two-bedroom, two-bath condominium in La Habra, California. I had a successful career as a consultant in the IT field, and I was teaching part-time at a local high school; yes, I am accredited to teach high school.

I felt healthy and fit mentally and physically, and at thirty-eight, I felt like I was on top of the world. Relationships with family and friends were strong. I finally felt like life was going my way. I could travel and had two cars in the garage, a roof over my head, and food in my belly. (I love food.) I met my now ex-wife at a funeral, of all things—I know, like a scene out of *Wedding Crashers*. However, neither my ex-wife nor I were directly related to the dead guy in the casket.

Rinse, lather, and repeat; those crazy cardinal-colored glasses blinded me to my ignorance. Wife #1 was different from the previous relationships in my life; she had a good resume, owned her own home (which later turned out to be untrue, maybe, I'll elaborate on that later), was educated and held a degree, drove a nice car, and was a flight attendant for one of the major airlines.

At our age, it's no surprise that she was divorced from a previous marriage and had no children. *OK, so she checks most of the boxes. Maybe this one won't drain me emotionally?* In chapter one, I mentioned that I subscribed to the happy wife, happy life mantra. Again, I repeat, it is bullshit! In the wake of this relationship, I sold myself out to the devil, again not calling Wife #1 the devil. However, I gave everything in pursuit of what I thought was happiness.

After three short years, I proposed to Wife #1, and I was well on my way to becoming a husband, a provider, and a head of household. I was fucking wrong. I liked the idea of being needed. This is where my Captain-Save-A-Whore (CSAW) mentality kicked in. Wife #1 is not a whore, nor is she the devil, so before you write the publisher and complain, CSAW is a trap that many men fall into. Most fall into it at a young age, but in my case, it's a fucking lifelong habit.

Getting back to the story . . . In the span of five very short years, I gave away everything. I sold one of my two cars, left the teaching gig, gave away my consulting business, sold my condominium in Orange County, and moved to San Diego only to acquire a house with both our names on the title and only my name on the mortgage. (At this point, you have to ask yourself what kind of a financial "genius" would make such poor financial decisions.)

Finally, I got a job working in a cubicle—another form of self-imprisonment. I digress. The following two years weren't all that rosy. I began to see cracks in the relationship. My health began to decline, having had a shingles attack at thirty-eight. WTF? Shingles is an old-people's issue (The agist would say! Shout-out to Gutfeld!). Apparently not. Stress was at an all-time high, gaining weight, drinking habitually, and building one hell of a resentment toward the person I was supposed to "love."

At this point, I have to break away and say that every one of us humans has narcissistic tendencies. Most of us are able to recognize our own contribution to narcissism and quickly correct those behaviors, which, in turn, does not make us narcissists. Follow me here; it's getting deep. Wife #1 was also lovingly referred to by her own family members as a "hurricane." She had a tendency to walk into a room and shake shit up, and as quickly as she arrived on the scene, she left, leaving a trail of wreckage behind and not taking any responsibility for the shitstorm she created. That's exactly how I felt after we divorced. Having sold our home after two years in San Diego, we relocated to Northern California to be closer to her family.

In May of 2018, Wife #1 and I divorced; for the most part, the divorce itself wasn't financially expensive, and I am genuinely thankful for that. I refinanced the home we were living in and cashed her out, and we split what little assets we had. For the most part, the divorce was amicable. We had no children, so no child support or alimony was claimed from either side, nor was it required.

Until it came down to our beautiful dog Olly (purposely spelled that way), that is when the ugliness really came out. During that time, I was an active member of the California State Guard; our primary function was to support the citizens of California in times of emergency. Anyone living in California for any length of time is well aware of fire season, then flood season, and mudslide season. Yes, we have seasons for disasters in California. In July 2018, I was called in to support the fire effort in Northern California. At this time, Wife #1 was living with her parents, and we were splitting custody of Olly.

It worked out well for a little while. When I was deployed, Olly would stay with Wife #1 at the ranch (her parents' home), and when I returned and she needed to go to work, Olly would stay home with me—until communications between Wife #1 and I began to decline and become scarce. When I did receive a text message, the messages would be hostile, warning me to stay away from the ranch and not bother my ex-in-laws. I was no longer welcome to visit Olly. It was tough. Olly was the only line item neither of us stipulated on the divorce papers.

I had to lawyer up, and now most of you would say it's just a dog. Hell, I've even uttered those exact words when speaking to pet owners—until I had a loving friend in my life like that dog, the true definition of unconditional love. Olly was my baby boy. Unable to have children for myself, and a low sperm count (too much soy and beer in my life), Olly was and always will be my best friend. (A boy and his dog.)

The most upsetting part about the divorce and the custody battle was how far Wife #1 would go to prove a point.

While going through the court proceedings, I warned my attorney that Wife #1 is the type of person that will dig her heels in to prove a point many times, doubling down even when she is in no position to contradict. During court, she had three family members under oath present affidavits regarding my character as a human being. The disturbing part is that it was scripted—like many child custody battles in family court. The most hurtful statement was from my ex-father-in-law. He lied in the interest of his daughter. I guess it is to be expected. I worshiped and held my ex-father-in-law in high regard; I was crushed.

Again, having too high of expectations of humans is the quickest way to disappointment. Although we were only family by marriage, I still felt that slap of betrayal. My father-in-law and I had many conversations over menudo about life, marriage, and family. He seemed to have it all together, later only to realize that he was only human. Damn you, expectations! I hadn't realized, even at this point in life, that placing people on a pedestal will always lead to disappointment. In some way, I was looking for a father figure that I never had. For the most part, my now ex-father-in-law is a good man, but he is fallible. He is human.

In October of 2018, Wife #1 had closed escrow on a home in San Diego; her intent was to leave Olly with her parents at the ranch. If she intended to move back to San Diego and take Olly with her, then such is life. Goodbye, my handsome boy. However, Olly was not nor will ever belong to her parents. She had no legal right to give Olly away to her parents when I was home and could care for him.

By the end of our marriage, I believe that Wife #1 and I had grown indifferent. What we both thought in the beginning to be love, simply wasn't. We grew apart. I had a fantasy in my head, thinking that marriage would be the partnership I had always wanted. It turned out to be a thousand concessions (shout-out to Rich Cooper) until I no longer recognized the person looking back at me in the mirror. I lost myself to an idea that wasn't my own, an idea that is sold to many men, that there is one person on the planet who would complete me. Fuck you, Jerry Maguire! I won the court custody case and brought Olly home with me on May 17, 2019.

I mentioned in the last paragraph concessions; I conceded myself and sold everything in my life to ensure my counterpart's life was comfortable. This goes against everything that I am—a hedonist. There was little to no pleasure, and the marriage quickly became uncomfortable on many different levels. I disallowed myself my own comforts and pleasures and sacrificed them to someone else. As a result, my financial, emotional, and physical health declined. I lost my frame; I lost me. This is what hell is. It's not a sharp-looking fellow with a pointed tail and horns. It is selling yourself out.

I short-changed myself for the pursuit of love; the fucked-up thing is, when looking at the guy in the mirror, I was entirely at fault. Before marriage, I had a small window where I was on my game. I respected myself, and I was able to look at myself in the mirror.

Psychologically, physically, financially, and professionally, I was in good health and was coming into a wholeness that was me. I was building a frame, a foundation to build upon. I let it all go for the idea that someone else could fulfill me when, simply put, only I can fulfill my needs, or soul, for that matter.

At the end of our marriage, there was no love. Indifference was all that was left. The marriage had become sexless, which was the beginning of my addiction to porn. I began a habit of masturbating compulsively, specifically when she was working. Fantasizing about other women and porn stars, the more I watched porn, the more depraved and sadistic the pornography I was seeking got. After Wife #1 left the house, dating apps became the avenue to feed my addiction. I looked specifically for hookups and then realized how negatively the porn addiction had affected my libido—just another layer of hell I've sunken to.

These are some questions to consider if you're living in your own personal hell:

1. How many times have you sold yourself out?

2. How many times have you conceded to avoid an argument?

3. How many times have you compromised and felt like you've received the shit end of the stick?

Compromise and communication, I've tried that approach, including couples/marriage therapy. The result was that the couple's counselor appreciated me and my willingness to participate, and my ex-wife felt threatened. For a relationship to work, both parties need to be 100 percent responsible for it. That means looking in the mirror and recognizing the part you play in the drama. I don't hate my ex-wife; actually, I have to thank her, again being another pivotal piece in my growth on my journey in life.

Girlfriend #1 . . . this is where all my distorted views on relationships began. This one is going to be a bumpy ride. This nine-month relationship is my first lesson in CSAW; I was all of twenty-one years old . . . yep, we are going way back, thirty years back. This is when my penis actually cooperated with my will. (Youth is wasted on the young.) The relationship with Girlfriend #1 was nothing but fucking, every day, day in and day out. It was all primal. There was nothing romantic about this relationship, just sex.

Girlfriend #1 was twenty-five, a single mother, an exotic dancer (stripper), and worked in a local hole in the wall in the City of Industry, an industrial part of Los Angeles County. She had a great set of legs, and chemistry (lust) was all over the place. We would have been fucking on stage if given a chance. Girlfriend #1 brought nothing to the table other than excitement. It's always the crazy ones that rock you in the bedroom. Girlfriend #1 was the right kind of crazy. We fucked in helicopters, military vehicles, movie theaters, and the back seat of a car in broad daylight as my friend drove us to the next party. Public and private venues, it didn't matter. I was pussy whipped.

Like all the other relationships in my life, it soon fell apart. Now, I could let myself off the hook and say I was seduced; I didn't know any better; I was naive, or young, dumb, and full of cum. I don't remember much of what was going through my head at the time (vagina).

What I do remember is that the longer I was around Girlfriend #1, the shittier I felt. We drank and partied constantly. There were always other men in the picture, sometimes directly and sometimes indirectly. Girlfriend #1 was a hustler, a man-eater and she played all of us like a fiddle. I had consistent access to her vagina in the nine months we were together, and I am pretty sure others did too. This is speculation on my part and I could be totally wrong. (No, I'm sure she was a proper garden tool.) The other men in her life could have been just sugar daddies; again, most of the evidence I have is speculative at best.

However, there were those times when my buddy or I would drive Girlfriend #1 and her "girlfriends" to "private parties." There is no doubt that she was a hooker (sex worker) in order to make ends meet. She had to be getting money somewhere, because I sure as shit wasn't making any real money to sustain myself, much less a single mom and her child.

Regardless, I was her personal bouncer, her muscled simp, waiting in parking lots after shows. Total cliché, such a shitty experience for all parties involved. Again, I don't blame her in any way, shape, or form. It was a lifestyle I actively participated in. The experience taught me what red flags were. While I never paid any money to her directly, but I paid with my soul. The perception of sex, relationships, and intimacy were all skewed in the negative, and I, as well as future relationships, would suffer because of these experiences.

It was adolescents running wild. This relationship only solidified my negative self-esteem for the years to come. I wasn't good enough for a stripper. Therefore, in my thinking at the time, I wouldn't be good enough in future relationships.

That's a difficult hole to crawl out from, the damage I had done to myself. During the course of that relationship, I contracted a venereal disease. (Chlamydia, such a beautiful name. I think I'll name my daughter Chlamydia, shout-out to the movie *Waiting*, 2005.) I can speak about this now because I feel this contributed to my low sperm count. Now this could be considered a blessing when logic kicks in, and I ask myself today, why the fuck would you want to have kids at fifty?

By the time this relationship had ended, I had solidified my career in alcoholism. I drank to forget about everything, my self-esteem was in the dirt, and I had no idea what to do.

By the age of twenty-two, I racked up two driving under the influence (DUI) charges and pissed away any chances of going to flight school. I hated myself so much I contemplated and attempted suicide. Obviously, I couldn't go through with it. There was too much I still wanted to do. A loser by every definition, lying on my mom's couch, I knew there was something better; I just didn't know how to get there. (See what I did there. I wrapped the ending of this chapter with the beginning of the first chapter.)

In every relationship between Girlfriend #1 and Girlfriend #5, I was looking for approval and wanted to be part of the clique—not much different than high school, always wanting to belong. So I wrapped myself in a warm vagina; I have to thank every woman that has graced my path. In repeating my juvenile behaviors over and over again, I learned about myself each time. The lessons keep coming; as long as I am breathing, I'm sure the Old Man Upstairs has a few more lessons for this knucklehead.

Before you go on judging me, take a minute to contemplate how many times you've sought approval. Approval is addictive because it doesn't come around often. When approval does come, we get a dopamine hit. So the next questions to ask yourself are as follows:

1. Whose approval are you seeking, Daddy's, Mommy's?

2. Whose affirmation are you looking for when you post your cleavage on Instagram?

3. What validation are you craving?

4. Whose approval were you looking for when you posted the picture in front of the private jet you never flew in?

Chapter 5

Growth and a Different Perspective

Fast-forward a few years . . . Girlfriend #5 version 2.0 . . . (aka, Girlfriend #6).

I'll be the first one to admit it, I am a sucker for vagina. Now I understand what you are thinking. How could I possibly reduce women to their genitalia? I'm not; however, since modern and extreme feminism has taken root in Western society, it has become clear that women no longer require men, and in kind, men have responded.

The only thing that is required is the need for sex. Procreation these days is an idea of the past and no longer serves a purpose, not even to propagate the species (according to modern feminism). And now, as of this writing, the trans-activists and large genome corporations are monetizing procreation. Soon, if not already, we will have order up baby drivethroughs. Think I'm joking, follow the fucking money. Women are selling their children and themselves out for equanimity. (Stupid fucks.)

Over the last decade or so, there has been a significant shift in Western culture. In general, women have been indoctrinated into believing that men are insignificant. Men are no longer required for women to lead fulfilling lives. Most of the legal systems are biased toward women. And the Big Daddy Government can now fill the role of protector and provider. Every woman is strong and independent, and the traditional role of men no longer applies.

Take Girlfriend #6, for example, a recent relationship and adventure I embarked on. She is a powerful free thinker, gorgeous in her own right. A successful real estate agent, she is an independent woman who doesn't require much other than entertainment from men.

However, with technology, she had embarked on many dating adventures utilizing whatever dating app, fill in the blank. She shared with me a few stories and nightmares she had experienced. And much like many experiences shared by women, she couldn't find her Prince Charming. Again, at the risk of sounding redundant, the Prince Charming myth is bullshit. He doesn't exist. Look at Harry. He is a prince denounced by his family and is a complete SIMP. I digress.

Girlfriend #6 and I met out in the wild, and the relationship began hot and heavy. Obviously, there was a mutual attraction. Girlfriend #6, a forty-something powder keg of sexual explosiveness, was totally my type, sexy, confident, and chock full of narcissistic tendencies.

The relationship ended as quickly as it started. In a matter of ten days, we had two arguments where our conversation led to being hung up on. Clearly, Girlfriend #6 had no respect on any level for me as a man. This falls right in line with the mindset that modern women have. I also believe that men, in general, have the same mindset. People have no respect for one another, even at a basic human level.

When conversations, specifically tough conversations, end in hang-ups or getting shut down, obviously, the emotional intelligence of the person doing the hanging up is below average, still operating at the high school level. It's rude and inconsiderate, especially if a couple tries to establish a long-term relationship (LTR). So what caused Girlfriend #6 to hang up on me?

We were attempting to arrange a date night, going to an outdoor concert in the park scenario. In addition, Girlfriend #6 was trying to coordinate a triple date scenario with her girlfriends (red flag), each woman showcasing the ponies (men in their life). However, there was a glitch. Two out of the three women were having issues with their ponies, and Girlfriend #6 would be the only one bringing said pony (me) to the show.

Now this was a Tuesday. In the morning, I started on my routine. I checked into work, attended my morning meetings, and went on my twelve-mile bike ride. This is a routine that I have established for myself since the advent of the Covid pandemic. After breakfast, I contacted Girlfriend #6 to begin planning the date night. However, after disconnecting from the call, I had a feeling in my gut that "something" was not right with the world. My Spidey senses were tingling. I reached out via text and shortly after called Girlfriend #6. I mentioned that I wasn't feeling right about how we ended the conversation and asked Girlfriend #6 what was wrong.

She said she was expecting a text from me in the morning and was upset that I waited till noon to reach out. As I listened intently, she grew more frustrated because I couldn't understand why this was important, nor was Girlfriend #6 able to explain why she was growing increasingly upset. The conversation grew in intensity, and she told me that her previous boyfriends would always be the first to text in the morning (a red flag, being compared to previous relationships). I quickly responded, "Look at where those relationships ended?"

Now, you may think this was a cruel response. However, it was an accurate response. All the simps that catered to her whims did not last. When I met her, she claimed to be "single," so logically, every man she had dated before me had not satisfied her ego. Women, in general, when confronted with the truth, will almost always revert to emasculation or gaslighting in conversation; Girlfriend #6 was no different. (Before you, the reader, get your panties in a bunch, yes, we know you are the exception to the rule; we're not talking about you, obviously.) Generally, women will always compare you to prior relationships, hold you in comparison to their father if they grew up with a father, and attempt to break you down.

By comparing you and your personality with good and bad traits from former lovers in their lives, women want to ensure your concession by leveraging your ego against you.

NOTE: This also leads to high body counts, and that is why it's essential for you to understand her body count and, more importantly, your body count (more on this later).

Back to Girlfriend #6, I had to stop the conversation and get clarification, and I asked, "So allow me to understand. You want me to change who I am so you can feel good about yourself?" Her response was, "Don't bother coming tonight!" Click.

My recommendation is to remain stoic and not feed into this trap. Don't concede. Once you bend the knee and cater to the ego of women (or anyone, for that matter), you've compromised your integrity. This is very unattractive for women as much as men. If a woman wants to be in your life, she will be. Otherwise, consider yourself lucky; you've just avoided a train wreck.

Back to why body count is important for both men and women. If it is in your mind that you want to find a relationship, whether that be marriage, a long-term relationship (LTR), or a live-in situation, I highly recommend vetting your potential partner. Give it at least ninety days before jumping into bed with this person. I can hear the player community just about shitting themselves and responding with the same old notes from 1989, "If she doesn't put out by date three, then dump that bitch." Look, if you are playing the field and just looking for pussy, have at it. Plow as many fields as you wish. What I'm talking about is vetting the candidate for a relationship.

Follow me on this line of reasoning. I'll use the example of a corporation; most potential employees have a 90- to 180-day vetting period prior to becoming full-time with benefits. This is to ensure the corporation's new hire is a right fit for the culture of the work environment. Think of yourself as a corporation, and vet your LTR prospects. Most people will reveal themselves, and their true nature will naturally come out within the first ninety days. So if your potential LTR asks you to change your routine, to change the things that make you great and give meaning to your life, to accommodate her or his need for attention, then you know it's a red flag. Most candidates will eliminate themselves if you are paying attention, and no need to feel down on yourself. It isn't you. It's them.

Something else to consider is most people, in general, don't realize they are behaving badly, so it doesn't make sense to try to point it out. Simply excuse yourself from the situation. You can say something like, "This is no reflection of who you are as a human being. However, this relationship isn't going to work for me. I wish you the best of luck." And then bounce, get the fuck out of the situation.

How does the body count fit into this conversation? Well, it doesn't. However, if a woman has a high body count, it gives her ammunition to compare you to men she's previously fucked. She'll hold you to a standard you won't be able to satisfy because she is stricken with "alpha widow" syndrome (I think Rollo Tomassi coined that phrase). Much like Girlfriend #5 and Wife #1, Girlfriend #6 compared me to her prior relationships. A woman with a high body count will compare you to Tyrone Thundercoque the minute you disappoint her, or she believes she has been disappointed. She won't come out and say it, but she is thinking it, all while swiping through her dating apps, looking for the next guy. The ninety days will allow you to see if her garage is clean and organized. (Again, no pun intended.)

Your body count should be at least in the double digits. This is important. Men must understand and navigate a woman's vagina and how to pleasure her. How to do this is outside the scope of this book. You'll just have to wait for my next book, where I will share all my dirty little secrets. However, my logic is sound. After she gets home from her date with "Beta Bucks," she'll be calling you for the "Alpha Fuck" (shout-out to Rollo). Your ego will thank me. They always call back at least once!

Hot mess! Girlfriend #7 was a twenty-eight-year-old train wreck. This experience was nothing but red flags written all over it. I just have to lay it all down, sexy brunette with a nice little body, but green highlights, tattoos, piercings, single mother, daddy issues, and a taste for whiskey (all red flags). Talk about a party on wheels. Going into this experience, I wasn't expecting much. With that being said, there was a significant age gap. Typically, in most situations, I am the life of the party. Naturally, people tend to gravitate toward me. Don't expect too much from younger women if you're an older gent. They have very little to bring to the table regarding life experience. Yes, the sex was fun, but that's about all. I have to caveat that last statement; if you are looking for marriage and children, then younger women will fulfill the requirements. However, be cautious and vet your candidate.

One thread I've noticed in most of my experiences regarding sex is that there is a propensity to steer toward shared trauma. As I began to learn more about these women, I found we shared traumatic experiences in our lives. Some of the women are pursuing help through therapy or coaching. However, not all therapists are created equal; back to shared trauma, I had my fair share of trauma in my youth, and I've painstakingly tried to heal from those wounds most of my adult life. In my experience, I'm OK with women sharing their traumas. It doesn't scare me. What I am sensitive to, and I ask the question, is, have they done the work and changed their victim mindset?

These are the red flags every bachelor needs to be aware of. If you get involved with an individual who has not reconciled with their past, you will be the target of blame for every trauma they've experienced in their life (Girlfriend #5). No amount of "Captain Save a Whoe" energy will save her.

One of the biggest things that tipped me off regarding Girlfriend #7 was that early on, love bombing (red flag) was in full gear. In addition, she told me that she wouldn't lie to me (red flag). This is a huge red flag in any situation. If a man or woman is telling you what they won't do in advance, the probability is high that is precisely who they are. Again, they might not be aware of their character defects. In this situation, they may not consider a "white lie" a lie.

Ultimately this short-lived excursion ended with me being lied to. The details aren't necessary. However, most people will tell you who they are in simple conversation. You just need to listen to it. Simps do it all the time. They tell you everything they are not and end up being exactly who they warned you about. That's coming from a reformed simp.

There is a common thread regarding all the women in my life. They all happened to be fucking fast. It was zero to sixty in sex and instant gratification. Don't get me wrong, it's in a man's biology to pursue sex as a driving force for propagating the species. The lizard part of our brain has a vagina (or sex) at the forefront. To add some perspective on the "lizard brain," it's any part of a person's psyche or personality dominated by instinct or impulse rather than rational thought.

Where men have an instinctual need to fuck, women have the instinctual need for security and resources. Deny all you want; this is how humans were programmed. Add into the mix social pressures, past experiences, positive and negative, and the need for instant gratification (this is a big one). Now you have a dynamite and nitroglycerin cocktail just ready to cause chaos. Some relationships move like a slow-burning fuse. Some burn faster, and eventually it all blows up in your face. It is difficult enough just to take care of one's own needs, much less to take care of your counterpart's psychological needs.

Coming full circle to what was mentioned earlier, women no longer need men to fulfill their need for security and resources. They are either employed or have Big Daddy Government subsidizing and filling this role. The modern wave of feminism has also taught women that they can fulfill physical needs through other women. And dating apps make it much easier for women to increase their body count.

On the contrary, the men who are still men and self-sustaining by their own contributions—own property, pay bills, and are generally responsible—are overlooked because these values are no longer valued. What to do?

Well, there have been many movements over the last twenty or so years, Men Going Their Own Way (MGTOW), Red Pill vs. Blue Pill, and Black Pill (I have no idea what this is, and it doesn't matter), proving men are disengaging. And feminists are having a shit fit; women are freezing their eggs to pursue careers, forgo family, and live adventurous lives. It's an interesting dichotomy; young women are seeking happiness and fulfillment, simping themselves to an ideological cult mindset, and all the while, they are experiencing stress and depression at alarming rates. At the same time, men are being men and doing what they've always done.

On the other side of that coin, there is the player movement, men trolling the internet and dating apps to get as much pussy as possible, increasing their own body count. An entire industry has been built around the player mindset of getting laid as much as possible without the need for commitment, tearing through the up-and-coming talent (college-age women) and leaving nothing but carnage in their wake. And as a result, most young women have a body count of ten or more men by their sophomore year in college. (Burn the bra, yay!)

I myself have been accused of being a player. However, I believe I've been miscategorized. If you are going to label me and put me in a box, then make sure you have all your facts straight. I am not a player; players manipulate and lie to get between a woman's legs. (I realize this contradicts chapter 2, so allow me to clarify: simps typically fixate on the one object of their desire, where players have multiple targets.) Today, I will tell you that I openly date women, sometimes simultaneously, sometimes one at a time. This is also known as *spinning plates*. I have a pallet for vagina, but I won't cheat; however, cheating is defined nowadays, and it's a subjective term. I no longer play the role of a good friend to women I want to fuck. You could say I am a reformed simp!

In the last two chapters, I laid out (no pun intended) some of my early relationships and, in contrast, some of my later escapades. In doing so, I wanted to illustrate the shift in thinking and approach regarding relationships. Where in early relationships, I was all too eager to get into a commitment with whoever was available, simp mindset, in the latter ones I was intentionally vetting prospects. Yes, I still love women and vaginas. My libido is still intact. However, I am way more selective. Believe me, if there is an opportunity to smash, won't look a gift horse in the mouth. However, fucking after the third date, well, it's meaningless and fruitless. Today I willingly vet and take my time. While easily grazing o low-hanging fruit is fun, I'd rather establish a foundation to develop a relationship with worthwhile prospects. Hopefully, avoiding chaos and headaches, stoicism plays a considerable role in keeping you sane.

As of this writing today, I've also considered abstaining from sex altogether; it seems that while spinning plates is fun, dating takes resources. I also have to think about what kind of a return I am getting for the simple act of fucking. Remember, time, energy, money, and resources are finite. I consistently ask myself, what type of woman am I welcoming into my frame?

Here is a simple truth I have also discovered in dating: "normies" cannot date people who are in recovery programs (of course, there are exceptions, so don't get your underwear all bunched up). After having dated people who do not understand the principles of the twelve steps and are not even curious enough to ask or show any interest, I realize the probability of these relationships lasting is low.

Chapter 6
Victimhood vs. Happiness

If I could bottle happiness, I would be a millionaire ten times over. Or, in today's numbers, a billionaire. I honestly believe that the more money you have, the more the potential for happiness decreases exponentially. In addition, having tons of wealth will only exasperate the douchebag you already are. Money, in general, buys freedom; I do believe this. Just look at today's court systems. The individuals who have money bog down the court systems and pay minimal retributions. In contrast, the average human gets raked over the coals—in my case, forced into indentured servitude until I satisfied the retributions society asked of me. This takes time, a lot of fucking time! Time I can't get back.

I believe that billionaires today have more headaches than they know what to do with. Most regular folks aren't cut out to manage one hundred thousand employees worldwide. In addition, I don't believe that most humans, including yours truly, have the intestinal fortitude to withstand the scrutiny most billionaires endure. Some billionaires are so narcissistic that they need to funnel their money into pandemics under the illusion of philanthropy to keep themselves entertained (shout-out to Bill Gates and George Soros!).

Happiness was defined to me in terms of happenings, meaning that most humans are waiting for something to happen to feel happiness. Examples include graduating high school or college, buying a new car, wrapping one's happiness in a new promotion or a fucking wedding, or correlating their happiness with the purchase of a giant home, not to exclude having the perfect wife or husband and basing all their happiness on the image these trophy humans provide.

We as humans wrap our very existence into outside stimuli and mind fuck ourselves into thinking that these are the things that make us happy. We consistently seek happiness by cultivating and collecting people, places, and things. I did it! I am a goal-oriented person; I chased certifications, degrees, jobs, money, cars, and women, thinking that the next one and the next one would "make" me happy. The mindset that objects of my lust and desire would make me happy only stood to make me miserable.

Around my mid-forties, a shift started to take place, just before my divorce, having had the two cars in the garage, a four-bedroom house (for a party of two, what a waste), the flight attendant wife, and a career in public service. You would think life was perfect. The reality: I was actually a slave, a slave to the system, purchasing objects to keep up with the neighbors. I was a slave to bills, a slave to my significant other's whims, and a slave to creditors. None of these things made me fucking happy. I was fucking miserable chasing someone else's definition of happiness.

Shortly after the divorce, I began to think of those few moments I believed I was happy (or joyful). I began to think back to when I owned a nine-hundred-square-foot condo, owned my consulting business, taught at a local high school part time, ate right and exercised on the daily, and finally, was free to meet and engage in meaningful relationships with all people from all walks of life.

Chasing objects, marriage, and money didn't bring me happiness. I began to realize that quality of life, how I defined quality of life, is what truly brought joy into my life. Towards the end of my marriage, we began to grow indifferent toward each other, both realizing that this partnership was a fantasy built on bad ideas.

Two years after my divorce, I remember an evening lying in bed after sex when I was asked by Girlfriend #5, "Do I make you happy?" My answer: "My happiness is not your responsibility; only I can make myself happy."

It was a profound answer, to be sure. There are few moments when a woman can get a sincere answer out of a man, and it's typically after sex or a half bottle of Jack Daniels. With that said, my understanding of this line of questioning was as follows:

1. She was looking for validation and purpose.

2. At least at that moment, her self-worth was contingent upon my yes answer.

3. Her question had nothing to do with me and my happiness.

The correct way to ask that question is, "Are you happy right now?" This takes the "I" out of the first question and conveys a genuine interest in me with the "You" in the question.

As I understand it now, happiness is an emotion we feel in between other emotions, much like love. It is not a complete state of being. Humans are happy, sad, angry, scared, or ashamed. I am sure you can add a few more feelings to that list. The point is that happiness is derived from inside of you. One cannot give or receive happiness from outside influences.

How many people have you heard say, "I don't like surprises?" Yet their significant other plans a surprise party in an attempt to make them happy. What could be so wrong with a party, especially a surprise party? Yet the target of the surprise party, after being confronted by forty guests yelling, "SURPRISE!" blows a gasket and storms off, furious. In most circumstances, a surprise party would be fun and may induce happiness or joy, but not to all people, as emotions are subjective. So never assume you make other people happy. You do not have that much power. In addition, never assume that you can control someone's grief.

Individuals feel the feelings they feel. We have feelings. It's all part of being human. However, each individual has the power within themselves to generate anger, fear, joy, or shame. With that understanding, then, it must also serve to be true that we can balance these emotions within ourselves. This concept was one of the hardest pills to swallow. My ego and self-talk couldn't handle that blow early in my life. What do you mean it's up to me to make myself happy? What do you mean it's not my father's, mother's, friend's, wife's, girlfriend's, boss's and the rest of society's responsibility to cater to my feeling and make me happy? My ego and construct wanted to blame everyone else for my problems, the political environment, the news outlets, everything except the common denominator: the guy staring back at me in the mirror. The problem was when I looked in the mirror, I couldn't look at that guy staring back. I hated him, didn't like who he was, and didn't want anything to do with him.

I have a pretty impressive resume, none of which means much to me personally. Most of my accomplishments were done for the approval of someone else. By the way, he died, and I never received the approval I was looking for. The things that meant the most to me were small accomplishments, having built a consulting business, having a few photos published in a local magazine, teaching and sharing my knowledge of the industry, cooking and sharing a good meal with friends and family, and finally, getting around to writing this book.

As I am hammering away at these keys and sharing my experiences, I feel a great sense of joy. Most of the things that bring me happiness, I made little to no money on; they afforded me a roof over my head, food on the table—food that I could share with friends and family, and expressing ideas with intelligent, open-minded people.

Shout-out to Alex Hormozi, I think he articulated it best, "Find happiness and joy in the process of life, and stop looking at happiness as a destination or a goal." (Of course, I misquoted the shit out of what he said, but you get the point.)

Victimhood, I'll forego *Merriam-Webster*'s definition for now, but I will express my own definition: where a person or group places responsibility for their own state of being on another person or group. Let's unpack this idea for those readers who can't understand reading at the eighth-grade level. Victimhood is where you blame others for your lot in life. Now let's investigate *Merriam-Webster*'s definition of *victim*: "one that is subjected to oppression, hardship, or mistreatment; one that is tricked or duped." So it stands to reason that victimhood is when one chooses to live in a victim's mentality."

This truth was given not so subtly in a conversation that took place in my mid-thirties with a very dear lifelong friend around the summer of 2008. My friend Jim and I would frequent a local chain restaurant for drinks, cheap tacos, and karaoke. For weeks we engaged in conversations about life. These conversations typically revolved around me bitching about life and how things weren't going my way. The business was slow, my sex life sucked, my relationships with women were horrible, and I had gained too much weight—I complained about just about everything I could complain about.

For some time, I would dump all my shit onto Jim, until he finally told me he didn't want to hang out anymore! He looked at me and said point blank that he was tired of my complaining week in and week out. I was a fucking downer, always complaining about shit. He finished by saying, "If you don't like what's going on in your life, then fucking change it." He continued by saying I was the only one who could turn my circumstances around. He hated that I refused to take responsibility for my participation in my life.

Like any really good friend who genuinely cares and serves up an open-faced shit sandwich, he finished by reminding me of my attributes. He reminded me I am intelligent, a genuinely good person, and fiscally responsible and I had no room to complain about shit and circumstances I had no control over, again reminding me that the only thing I had control over was me and my perspective.

Talk about a slap in the face and closing with a big wet kiss. That was an aha moment. My victimhood is unattractive and served as a repellent. In general, most people don't like self-claiming victims and martyrs, mainly when one's victimhood is self-perpetuated. Actual victims, in my opinion, are ones that are inflicted with pain or grief outside of their control. Examples include acts of God or nature, including random events such as violent crimes to varying degrees.

However, it seems in vogue to be a victim these days—victims of circumstances entirely within our control. I mentioned earlier that I complained about being fat, overweight, obese, and unhealthy. Aside from an actual medical condition or some physiological ailment, I had to accept my role in my weight gain. Eating fast food three times a day and smoking two packs of cigarettes were all in my control. That supersized number two meal with a filet-o-fish fish on the side and sixty-four-ounce Coke was all on me.

I relished the idea of being a victim. It was way too easy to blame other people and events for the ills in my life. I loved the sympathy and attention that came along with playing the victim. Until playing the victim began alienating the people who were close to me. Until the bitching and complaining became unattractive. In one conversation, it became clear that victimhood was tearing me away from the people close to me—the people I respected.

Life does have its ups and downs; I believe every one of us can agree on that. It's what you do in the down times that define your character. In addition, life can remind us of lessons we have forgotten when we fall into familiar traps and forget what we need to do to lead productive lives.

Many years before the conversation with Jim, I had a similar conversation with my Uncle Mike. I honestly considered this man a mentor. I had an opportunity to spend a week with him on a road trip. He was relocating from Southern California to Virginia for work.

To paint some context, I was knee-deep in the relationship with Girlfriend #1, had a second DUI under my belt, had no driver's license, and was really feeling shitty about myself. I was down, no doubt. My uncle clearly did not want to be put in the situation of giving anyone advice. I believe he was coerced by my mom and her sister my aunt to have a conversation with me and set me "straight." However, I don't have any evidence that this is true. Nonetheless, we loaded the U-Haul and began the trip across the country. In proper form, I began bitching and complaining about how life sucked and blamed everything around me regarding my shitty circumstances.

I remember saying I needed a break, like life owed me something, thinking that life was to provide me with opportunities to rectify my circumstances, some fucking hero to rescue my ass from me. I liken it to wasting a week's salary on lottery tickets, exchanging tangibles for fantasy.

I'll never forget my uncle's response, "You make your breaks! You can't go through life expecting someone to save you from you." Those were the words I needed to hear: I have to change my circumstances. There is no one alive who can save me from me. I have to take responsibility for myself. I was starting my adult life at a deficit. My actions put me in the situation I was living. My actions determined my circumstances.

Now, I can hear all the arguments to the contrary, and most of these arguments will come from individuals who subscribe to victimhood. Critics will say, "You are white. You are a man. You're Christian, Anglo-Saxon," and whatever other excuse as to why I had better opportunities than others. To those same critics, I will provide you with some of my history. I grew up in a lower-middle-class immigrant family. (Yes, I am a first-generation American.) Most of the kids growing up in my neighborhood were from immigrant families, Hispanic, Black, Asian, Pacific Islander, and Armenian, and most were all first-gen Americans.

Their parents came to the United States, much like my own, and didn't have a pot to piss in, as most of our parents at the time were earning around $13.75 an hour, a median wage for that period (1986). Some were political refugees from South American countries fleeing under threat of death. So by all standards, financially, ethnically, politically, and socially, we were all in the same boat.

We all had an equal opportunity to become great and an equal opportunity to become shitheads (shout-out to Hunter Biden). The kids I grew up with in my neighborhood did outstanding in their lives and are all successful in their own right. To my knowledge, most busted their asses to become police officers, teachers, real-estate moguls, doctors, attorneys, fathers, and mothers and became better by all standards than the previous generation. Out of that class of men and women I graduated high school with, they took responsibility for themselves, educated themselves, and made their own breaks. I'll guarantee that none of them had an easy time of it. The hardest thing to do in life is to take responsibility for yourself; none of them subscribed to a victim mentality or blamed others for their shortcomings.

This leads me to this next generation of men and women. What the fuck is *woke*? Google defines *woke* as "past of wake"; the Urban dictionary Defines woke as "(Adj.) Being aware of current social issues. The word's meaning comes from the past tense of wake (I need to wake up/I just woke up). The phrase 'Wake up!' Here is a link, so you can look it up yourself: https://www.urbandictionary.com/define. php?term=Woke.

This is my definition of woke:

> Fascism disguised as social justice causes such as feminism, Black Lives Matter, Antifa (the irony), trans activism, and global activism, in addition to other social causes. Designed to divide and manipulate emotions to destroy the individual's right to autonomy, religion, and personal freedoms. Leveraging corporate and political influence to propagate a new world order, similar to Adolf Hitler and the Nazi Party. (Examples include Germany's political structure in concert with Bayerische Motoren Werke {Bavarian Motor Works}, Mercedes Benz, and Volkswagen in the 1930s.)

We know that mainstream media is bought and paid for by big tech and corporate giants. What do you think the MS in MSNBC stands for? Don't worry I'll wait . . .

Where am I going with this? Oh yeah . . .

We have a couple of generations of children who bitch and complain about everything. The younger generations (Gen Z) live to be victims. As mentioned earlier, even billionaires aren't happy, so they seek ways to entertain themselves at the expense of other individuals. They claim that social righteousness and virtue signal moral superiority. Yet they are malignant like cancer, degrading the foundations and principles this nation was built upon. Corporations and communist countries fund these social causes under the illusion of diversity, equity, and inclusion. Complete nonsense and bullshit! As a result, they march down streets and destroy property and lives, all in the name of what?

Do you remember how *Merriam Webster* defined *equity*? Certainly not how woke ideology defines it. Woke ideology rejects natural law and substitutes science with feelings. Fuck your feelings, you fuckin' worthless piece of shit! (Damn, that felt good! 😄)

As mentioned earlier, the woke ideology is the new face of Marxism. The irony is that the younger generations have no idea who Karl Marx or Frederick Engels is. I won't waste time explaining either. However, their ideas were born from a man who thrived under victimhood. Here is a little more irony: four out of his seven children died before the age of nine, and three of those children barely saw a year. The idea that everything in life should be free and the government should provide for the people is bullshit. It doesn't work! NOTHING IN LIFE IS FREE. There must be an exchange of effort in return for a reward (aka a transaction). NOTHING IN LIFE IS EASY. ANYTHING WORTH DOING IS GOING TO BE CHALLENGING.

The very same generation who claim that the Constitution of the United States of America and our Bill of Rights are old and antiquated is following the old and antiquated ideas of the father of victimhood himself, Karl Marx. That our youth are so willing to give up their autonomy, civil rights, and freedom for slavery, poverty, and socialism is a horrifying thought.

I can't blame them. I blame the previous generations (generation X, yes, my generation), who allowed for this change in our public institutions, culture, and communities under the false pretenses of tolerance. They only have to look at Venezuela and Cuba to see the results of Socialism. The following generations don't understand that this woke ideology seeks to destroy the middle class. This is the price a politically apathetic generation must pay. We (gen X'ers) fucked up.

This up-and-coming generation is simping about the idea of utopia, brotherhood, empathy, and free public service. These children have no idea that socialism and communism will only bring genocide, poverty, exile, injustice, and misery. There is no ROI where socialism and communism are concerned.

If you are truly unhappy with the world's state, only you can change it by changing yourself. If you live in a socialist state like California, New York, and Illinois, you can move out to a state that supports and defends the Constitution of the United States. You also have the power to turn off the TV and stop supporting the bullshit, subscribing to Amazon (the irony), Disney, and Netflix. Stop buying shit from China (I'm guilty of it too). Stop buying the products that you're loyal to. It's obvious these brands don't give a shit about your values. Stop simping to keep up with everyone else. You're obviously not gaining anything but losing everything. Stop shoving your social justice bullshit down everyone's throat and worry about you, you simple bitch!

If you do not like being fat, you drink too much, you can't seem to get your shit together, your relationships suck, and your boss is an asshole, take fucking responsibility for yourself and change yourself. The changes don't have to be huge. Start small and work your way up.

Five (5)

Do five individual things daily to change your life:

1. Do five pushups in the morning. If you can't do full-on pushups, do five chick pushups for a week and increase it to ten until you can do five regular pushups. Then increase that by five every week.

2. If you are tired of being fat, cut the sugar out of your life. This one is an all-or-nothing deal. If you want to cut weight fast, eliminate all the sugar in your life. That includes bread. Allow for one cheat day a month. (Cheat day doesn't mean stuff your fat fugly face with all the sugar you can ingest. Moderation is critical, even on a cheat day.)

3. Write down five things you are grateful for on a daily basis. If you have a roof over your head, be grateful you got a fucking roof over your head. Look at LA, SF, Oakland, and Sacramento. There are thousands of people who aren't doing as well as you.

4. If you don't like your job, find another job that suits you and your personality better, and then quit the shitty job. Don't quit first. Then you'll really be up shit creek. You may lose the roof over your head.

5. For all that is pure, stop playing the victim. No one cares about how you feel. The ones who pretend to care are only looking at you and are grateful they aren't as fucked up as you. (They laugh at how fucked up you are behind your back and talk all kinds of mad shit about what a colossal waste of space you are.)

6. And for fuck's sake, limit your exposure to social media. Reduce it to ten minutes a day. It's killing your brain.

Life can kick you in the teeth; hell, even the most savage of beasts have to lick their wounds occasionally. The question is, will you lie down and die, wallowing in your misery and self-pity, or will you persevere, learn from your miscalculations, and live?

> I guess it comes down to a simple choice, really: Get busy living, or get busy dying.
> —*The Shawshank Redemption*, 1994

Chapter 7
Finances and Work

As I mentioned in earlier chapters, I am a hedonist. I seek pleasure over pain. So it stands to reason that the idea of work (at least in my mind), well, sucks. I know many people on this planet enjoy work and are working in fields that bring them great joy. I am not one of those individuals. I do not enjoy working in a cubicle, and I do not like answering to a boss.

However, I did enjoy working as a consultant for thirteen years, until I traded freedom for security. I gave away my client list for an idea that wasn't necessarily my own. I take ownership of that decision because I made the decision, regardless of the circumstances that influenced that decision. Only in hindsight are the consequences of those decisions made clear.

Now, nine years later, I am in a job I don't enjoy, planning an exit strategy to get out of my current career situation. I enjoy the freedom of being a consultant. I enjoy addressing customers' technical needs and providing proper solutions to make these organizations profitable, efficient, and productive. Not one day is ever the same as a consultant. Literally, it is an adventure. You never know what challenges or needs a customer has from day to day.

From a financial perspective, I wasn't killing it. My lifestyle was very comfortable. My profession and the freedom it provided were invaluable. I truly enjoyed what I did. Please don't misunderstand. I had many seventy-two-hour weekends while performing fork-lift upgrades. (This term is used when completely overhauling a server room or infrastructure in an organization.) However, it was exciting, challenging, and fun. Physically and mentally, it worked. However, when you enjoy something, I liken it to playing—getting paid to play with very cool toys.

On the other side of that coin, I have been working in a structured environment for the last nine years. Working in a cubicle, the cubicle mindset isn't just your physical location within the building. When working for my organization, the operations aspect is siloed. I am restricted to a particular job function and forced to stay in my lane. Not fun, so I focus on different objectives to distract my mind.

The cubicle scenario is detrimental to my mental health and restricts my problem-solving skills and creativity. I'm boxed in—another version of hell. For most people, work is a necessary evil, but my attitude toward work is definitely negative. As mentioned earlier, I am working toward a solution. I need to be careful and calculate the risks. I need to work and, like many people in my situation, have bills to pay. So patience is required on my part.

As an IT consultant, I had many challenges and experiences. Most of my experiences were positive and allowed me to grow professionally, emotionally, educationally, and financially. I considered myself successful not based on my bank account, but on the freedom I enjoyed. I mentioned bills earlier, and I think this is an excellent segue into finances.

Before getting out on my own, I worked for an organization in Huntington Beach, CA, as an IT administrator. I made a better-than-average income for the period and learned much during this time. Staying true to my nature, I didn't like having to report to anyone. I didn't enjoy having a supervisor (at the time, I was directly reporting to the VP) who was less knowledgeable regarding technology. I didn't like answering to him or him telling me how to do my job. (Can you say ego?) I was relatively young, and my soft skills needed improving, no doubt. I had completed my undergrad program, been sober for a few years, and regained my privilege to operate a motor vehicle. By all counts, I was on top of the world for the time—until I found myself unemployed, returning to my college job as a bartender to make ends meet. Even the most savage of beasts have to regroup and lick their wounds. Sound familiar?

What was once the most incredible job while in school (bartending) quickly began to lose its allure. I wasn't making the same money as an administrator, and I had credit card bills, rent, car payments, etc. I quickly fell behind on my bills, struggling to make the car payments, and soon after couldn't make half of the rent. Then it happened; my mother called and asked what was going on with the credit card bill. A few years earlier, my mother had cosigned a credit card that I defaulted on, which was reflected on her credit report, and she almost lost the house she was trying to buy.

Just like that, ignoring responsibility, not having an exit plan, and allowing my ego to blind me, I was in deep financial shit. I couldn't get unemployment benefits; the Employment Development Department's (EDD) response was, "The terms under which you were dismissed could have been avoided."

FUUUUUCKK! I was fucked. I had no one else to blame (regardless of how much I tried to blame someone else). The most humbling time of my life was how I spent the next few years. By the grace of the Old Man Upstairs, I could find a job working the deli at a grocery store in Lake Forest, California. I crossed a picket line to get the job. Hell, I needed to get out from under this shit storm I had created.

At the time, I asked my girlfriend Dottie if she could loan me $333.10 to pay my car payment for that month. I then had to ask her father, Steven, if I could rent a room in his home until I could get on my feet again. It took about four years to move out. God bless Steve, Irene, and their family. They had a lot of patience with me. Then the credit card situation, well, Mom bailed me out. She had to. She had a deal to close. That was the most disappointing thing: She trusted me, and I let her down. I hated myself at that time, humiliated myself, and let down people close to me. I burdened others who had no real reason to help me. Only by the kindness and graciousness of others was I able to get back on my feet.

While working the deli gig, I looked for IT jobs and found one as a traveling computer technician, the precursor to the Geek Squad, long before Best Buy bought them up. This is where I thrived. There was a lot of freedom in being a subcontractor. At the same time, running a business was a steep learning curve. Going from a W-2 employee to a 1099 was a difficult transition. I knew nothing nor understood anything regarding filing quarterly taxes. I was a financial neophyte. The struggle was real when trying to start up my own business. The school of hard knocks is unforgiving, so you must align yourself with people who have done it before you.

Since my financial life was in disarray, I made a few invest-ments. QuickBooks to the rescue. The only problem was I had no clue how to use it. I know, you're asking, "How can a computer guy not know how to use a computer application?" The answer is simple, I can connect the front-end application to the database in the backend. I did that many times for customers. However, the accounting language used in the application was another discipline altogether.

Rich Dad Poor Dad by Robert Kiyosaki was a popular book at that time. I remember reading in the book (I won't attempt to quote it) about him looking for a financial guy and realizing that if he (Robert) was making money, then the finance guy would make money too. If Robert is reading this book, help a brother out and add some clarity to that last reference. I'll leave my contact info at the end of this book. With that advice, I searched for a good bookkeeper.

Loretta is the best; she has the mind of a teacher (shout-out to Dave Ramsey). In the beginning, she managed my books, helped me find a good tax consultant with a teacher's mind, and most importantly, taught me the nuances of QuickBooks. She showed me how to create accounts, draft invoices, reconcile accounts, and run P&L (profit & loss) and tax reports for the accountant. I'm not going to mislead you, the lessons were expensive financially. However, the lessons were invaluable. It's been several years since Loretta and I connected. She's retired now. However, I still use the application to this day in my professional and personal affairs.

In 2021, I was on the hunt for a new accountant. I am in the process of getting a new business venture up in addition to filing taxes, so having a good tax consultant is essential.

I found Michelle when I provided her itemized reports for my taxes, and I received the best compliment. My new accountant, Michelle, remarked, "I wish all my clients were this organized." I thank Loretta for teaching me the skills. The key point: find people who will provide you with an education, and pay them graciously for their knowledge. In turn, this will help you succeed.

There seems to be a common misconception that success is measured in monetary terms. This is a fallacy corporations want to sell to you. Success is subjective. You define what success is. For me, success is having good teachers in my life. This is how I was able to thrive despite my shortcomings.

I mentioned that in 2010, I purchased my first home in La Habra, CA. This was a crazy time for real estate, coming from a monumental financial collapse due to the subprime market and questionable lending practices. Banks had no direction; underwriters scrutinized every loan application like never before. They actually had to manually underwrite the loans juxtaposed to running them through automated software. Banks are in the business of making money, and the banks lost their asses between the period of 2006 and 2010. Stated income loans weren't a thing anymore, and I credit Loretta and her teachings that allowed me to provide the reports, financial history, and supporting documentation. That satisfied the underwriters and closed escrow in May of 2010. As a side note, Arthur at kinnectcapital.com, my real estate agent and close friend, was very patient with me—he explained and held my hand through the entire experience. Buying a home is an overly invasive process. As mentioned earlier, underwriters were scrambling and had to manually approve loans after dealing with the sub-prime fiasco.

Work and finances are a necessary evil. We use money to complete transactions for life, groceries, gas, and necessities, on top of all the luxuries we desire, leveraging our credit and making minimum payments, or in my case, being unable to make the minimums in 2005. I had a storage unit full of junk and creditors on my ass, and I was becoming a burden to my family and friends. This was not a happy time for me. During this period, the teachings of the twelve steps really began taking root; responsibility is vital.

Fast-forward twenty years later, I have a mortgage and no other debts. I don't consider myself frugal, but I understand what accounts receivable and accounts payable are. I do not make the mistake of paying out more than what is coming in. I leverage credit cards, although much like cash, it's a tool, nothing more. Through the lessons learned, I disciplined myself to reconcile all my accounts and keep a watchful eye on my spending habits. An old Sicilian proverb my dad shared with me in adulthood goes something like this:

> Only under the watchful eye of the owner will his
> horse grow.

There is something lost in the translation from Sicilian to English. The point is to keep an eye on your money and invest wisely in your endeavors, and you will see your wealth grow. Here are some things to consider moving forward:

1. Are you living a Ferrari life on a Yugo budget?

2. How are you contributing to the financial chaos in your life?

3. Is keeping up with your neighbors and social media important?

4. Everyone wants to be a rock star and live a glamorous life. How far in debt are you because you're chasing a fantasy?

5. What is your freedom worth? Are you willing to be enslaved by bad debt and credit cards?

BTW, a few years after I cleaned up my credit and had some cash readily available, I received a phone call from my mom. She was in distress. My sister, then going to college, had an issue with her Saturn SL1. The automatic transmission went out and needed repairs. My mom, living on a fixed income, didn't have the funds available. Strangely, the repair bill was equal to the amount I had defaulted on three years earlier. My sister's car was repaired, and my debt to my mom was paid in full. Interesting how the universe works. Thank you, Mom, for your patience. It took a little longer than anticipated, but I got there.

Chapter 8

Simping Is Not Restricted to Men Only

Obviously, I am not qualified to speak on a woman's behalf. Growing up for men and women is fundamentally different, regardless of how society defines a woman. (We will get into that subject later.) For now, we will stick with the concept of simping. As an observation, women are just as guilty of simping, though it isn't as overt as it is in men. To recap, men, in general, will dote on a woman to gain favor and eventually pussy.

Women also seek favor from other women and society as a whole to achieve acceptance. The whole feminist movement is structured around women not being good enough. So the movement was created to empower women and affirm the belief that a woman can do anything a man can do, while still caring for the family, being the breadwinner, staying sexually relevant, and maintaining youth. (HAHA! Joke's on you.)

Entire industries are built on the idea that women can do it all! Hold for shock face—you can't, no one can do everything and do it great all the time; this is the fallacy women subscribe to today. It is humanly impossible to juggle all of your life's demands, manage everything for children and family, and maintain your sanity. This is true for both men and women.

Sacrifices are made. Partnerships in raising and maintaining families are essential.

So how does a woman simp? They simp to each other, looking for acceptance, affirmation, and attention. Just as much as a man pays his hard-earned dollar on OnlyFools (shout-out to Joker), the woman on the screen is getting dollars, sure, but she is also seeking affection and affirmation, and she is willing to leverage her youth, beauty, and vagina for attention.

Women will simp to the millions of products that promise to improve beauty and maintain youth while seeking attention from others (men and women alike). Women seek out luxury, not necessity, while seeking security and engaging in promiscuity (the irony!) Products marketed to women alone are a multibillion-dollar industry. This marketing manipulates a woman's insecurity and convinces her to think she isn't good enough while the feminist movement continues to move the bar on what a woman is.

Matt Walsh did a documentary to define what a woman is (spoiler alert). Most of the women in his documentary couldn't define what a woman is. In this writer's opinion, this defines the mental state of women today. (The outlook is bleak at best.) You are the most powerful force on the planet. That little cock pocket between your legs is the only reason society exists. Throughout time, wars have been fought because some douchebag wanted to impress a woman (the mega-simp).

Women are losing their identities because of simping, in general not taking responsibility for some of the crackpot decisions they've made and blaming men for their insanity. The patriarchy, toxic masculinity, wage gap, blah, blah, blah, blah . . . all the while doing stupid shit and saying that men have shattered your self-esteem. This reminds me of a skit from *Pimp Chronicles pt. 1*, one of Katt Williams's genius stand-up shows. I will paraphrase because I'm a white guy, and writing the N-word or even a whisper of the word is frowned upon (just ask Joe Rogan). The bit goes something like this:

> Ladies, if you are twenty-five years old and still messing around with ain't shit "MEN," you need to get a handle on your life and take some responsibility. What you mean to say is that all the "MEN" you fuckin' with ain't shit! You need to figure out what it is about your pussy that keep attracting ain't shit "MEN."

This philosophy crosses all racial boundaries. This is just as true for black women as it is for white.

Women want to be taken seriously and looked at as powerful, skillful, and intelligent in the world. However, how can anyone take a woman seriously when she willfully gives her hard-earned money to hair and makeup salons (fake nails and hair extensions), performs cosmetic surgery to embellish parts of her anatomy, removes fat from other parts, gets fake eyelashes, and injects poison into her lips and forehead to appear youthful when she looks like a petrified deer in headlights (shout-out to Nancy Pelosi). Removing everything that makes a woman truly beautiful to the point where you look like hookers (no offense to the world's oldest profession) and clowns is perverted and distorted.

Then there are the women who overtly make themselves ugly. One of my favorite cultural fads (sarcasm intended) is the nose ring, the intentional piercing of the septum for facial embellishment. Here is some education I just learned, so I'll share it with you all. According to the American Mini Pig Association (AMPA)—"The metal ring piercing through the most sensitive part of a pig's body, the snout, will reduce rooting and damage to landscaping and lessen escape attempts."

Let's look at some more evidence. Here is another source you can look up from 4wileyfarm.com—"The bull ring has been used for generations as a safety measure to control an animal. The septum is a very sensitive area, so a tug on the bull ring will help to bring the animal into submission."

In both examples above, it is to subdue or control the animal, yet American women, who have freedom of choice and are independent, strong, stunning, and brave overtly advertise a symbol of control used on livestock and sell it as beauty. The irony is inescapable! Women who claim to be independent and strong put a tool in their noses that symbolizes submission and control. (Think about that.)

In human society and culture, "the septum piercing was used to signify their success and show their rite of passage into manhood," according to body-piercing.com. It also says that "the piercing of these flesh tunnels became connected to rebel subcultures such as the punk rock movement, which is seen as a sign of rebellion."

I get it, between the ages of eighteen and twenty-three, I went through a tattoo phase, and I still consider getting new ones. However, my ink is deeply personal, and I don't overtly show it off. However, I was thinking of the consequences when I did get my ink. I understood that the business world, in general, still, to this day, does not appreciate rebels with a delusional cause. I digress. Women want to be feminine but adorn themselves with jewelry customarily used for masculine tradition (more irony). Maybe my expectations are too high regarding culture today, as Matt Walsh poignantly points out, "What is a woman?"

I've always advocated the cliché, "You do you, booboo!" I must fact-check this, but I think Katt Williams coined that phrase too. However, in the wisdom of the great pimp himself, look in the damn mirror, take responsibility for yourself, and evaluate your participation in your stupidity.

Some final thoughts (opinions), coming full circle regarding attention, affirmation, and approval seeking. Stop posting cringe on social media. You are only attracting simps and other women who secretly laugh at you. They will use every bit of what you post against you. It may not be today or tomorrow, but the minute you change your perspective, they will call you a sell-out. However, if you continue buying into modern-day feminism, it is highly probable that you will suffer burnout and turn into the crazy cat lady down the street.

In short, men want virtuous women who complement their lives and bring peace and tranquility to the table. Most men don't give a shit if you have fake nails and hair extensions or a boob job. This behavior screams high fucking maintenance. However, there are a few Saudi princes that will gladly lavish you with gifts and money to watch you eat scat from a cup (shout-out to Man Talk).

On the other hand, if you are screaming that you bring a six-digit income or a degree in underwater transgender basket weaving and don't need a man, then you are just another form of competition in your man's world. I have to believe that most humans don't want to come home and be in competition with their partners. Most humans would much rather come home to a hug and a quicky before dinner. I think we can all appreciate that.

A little more on competing with the man in your life (or life partner, for that matter). Before my marriage, Wife #1, a good cook in her own right, prepared a traditional Mexican meal, complete with all the fixings. It was a delicious meal, to be sure, complete with Spanish rice, refried beans, and guacamole (the creamy sauce style)—delicious. The guacamole was a perfect fit for the meal.

A few months later, she hosted a party for her flight attendant friends. I was not at the event for one reason or another, most likely working—the details aren't necessary—but she had asked me to prepare my guacamole recipe (a chunky style for chips). The basic ingredients came from Tyler Florence on the cooking channel, and I added serrano chiles to make it my own. What I understood, according to Wife #1, was that her co-workers absolutely loved the guacamole and raved about the recipe. She went on to say that there were no leftovers, and it was the first food item to go.

Years later, during an argument, my wife accused me of being in competition with her and brought up the guacamole. I never considered my guacamole better than hers. As I said, her recipe was absolutely delicious. However, my wife harbored resentment (red flag ignored). The point of this anecdote is to look out for competing interests in your prospective partner. It will bite you in the ass later. I was never in competition with my wife. However, for some reason, she felt I threatened her with guacamole. BTW, for the first few years of our marriage, Wife #1 earned higher wages than I did after transitioning from consulting to a full-time employee. Competition was never an issue for me until it became one.

Chapter 9
Simping in General

Well, if truth be told, to some degree, we are all simps. We all want attention, affirmation, and approval and do foolish shit to achieve those goals. Unfortunately, you can please some people some of the time, but you can't please all the people all the time. Simping is part of the human condition—fuck!

I'm writing this book and simping for your attention, affirmation, and approval. Shit, I am willing to put my head on a chopping block and lay out some very intimate details to entertain you. Some of you may think this book deserves a Pulitzer Prize (not really), but most likely, it'll be used as toilet paper in the apocalypse. But we are all simping, parents simp to their kids, politicians simp to their constituents, corporations and governments simp back and forth to one another. Shit, Bud Lite simped to the transgender community and lost their asses in that deal—all the while thinking one controls the other for approval, attention, and affirmation. You know in your heart of hearts it's all bullshit.

If you really wanted to stop simping, man or woman, you would take complete and total responsibility for yourself. You would stop blaming your parents for not being rich (or being too rich) and raising you all fucked up. You would stop blaming the current political regime for fucking up the world. Poor people stop blaming the rich, and the rich blame the poor. Whatever your excuse is, stop making them. Take fucking responsibility, do yourself a favor, and contribute to your own fucking life. Make your bed, and stop expecting a reward for something millions of people do every day. And for God's sake, don't post that you made your bed on social media—#MadeMyBed.

It isn't easy recognizing your part in the world and the lack thereof, even when you claim that you didn't fuck up the economy! Really, during the worldwide pandemic when local small businesses shut down, did you support them? Did you stand up for them? Or did you stand up for an imaginary grandmother that pretty much stays at home and watches *The View*? Or maybe you took government funds designated to support small businesses during the pandemic when your business was doing fine? Or maybe you supported the big corporate giants and spent government funds not meant for you? Or you virtue signaled smoking a cigarette outdoors while wearing a state-mandated mask? I don't know. How were you contributing to that clusterfuck? What did you do? Did you loot and pillage the downtown businesses and contribute to all that damage during the summer of love? (Summer of Bullshit! The entire nation got conned by the mainstream media.) In my case, I drank and fucked myself silly for the better part of eighteen months.

I'm not innocent. I'm trying to take a look at how I contributed to the stupidity that transpired over the last three years (2020–2023). I know I should own stock at BevMo with the amount of alcohol I consumed. And as a result, I was diagnosed with a fatty liver, a precursor to cirrhosis. Who do

I blame for that one, Jack Daniels? Whom do I blame for my pussy appetite and the meaningless sex that transpired from those toxic relationships? You get the point—everything I did was to avoid taking responsibility for myself, and in doing so, I found myself miserable, alone, and unloved. Or at least it seemed that way.

In turn, I looked outwardly for affection, attention, and affirmation (aka, simping), which did everything to repel it. This is a shitty way to live; there is no glory in going to bed every night drunk as fuck and masturbating to shitty porn so you can get to sleep. All of my best thinking paved the way to my realization that there is a better way. How did I go from being a successful business owner with cash in the bank and a positive outlook on life to a morally bankrupt, drunken, and depraved human being? SIMPING!

Simping will destroy you, some faster than others, but ultimately you will be standing in the mirror and looking at yourself as a shell of your former self, asking, "What did I do?" In the short term, we may convince ourselves that we are getting away with shit, but ultimately, it all catches up. You may not even be there to see it, but you may only have the gravediggers and the local preacher at your funeral, not having impacted anyone positively in your life, much less your own.

OK, so how does one pull themselves out of this toilet spiral we call simping? In the introduction, *Meriam-Webster* defined a *simp* as a foolish or stupid person. Well, I certainly behaved in foolish and stupid ways over the years. We are all guilty of doing stupid and foolish shit. How else can you explain the '80s? The answer is as unique as you are. First and foremost, get some God (or, at minimum, spirituality. I'm not saying psilocybin hippie spirituality shit, I'm saying good old-fashioned read-the-Bible spirituality) in your life. I know, I can hear it now; here we go, another Bible thumper. No, what's important here is that there is something bigger than you that exists in your life. Fuck, make Jack in the Box (although not recommended) your higher power, something that holds you spiritually accountable. Think of something that you want to aspire to be from a virtuous perspective, something that embodies charity, gratitude, humility, chastity, temperance, patience, and diligence. This is important because this will help you get out of your narcissism, self-entitlement, and nihilism.

Then take a leap of faith and believe that whatever hole you dug yourself into, you can dig yourself out of. None of this is easy as it sounds, but diligence helps. Again, another cliché comes to mind, "How do you eat an elephant? One bite at a time." Take small steps to improve yourself. Jordan Peterson, in his book *12 Rules for Life, an Antidote to Chaos* suggests cleaning your room. In my opinion, this is a great start in taking small steps to improve your situation.

Storytime: In my early twenties, that small step for me was waking up and brushing my teeth. I was looking at a second DUI conviction and didn't have twenty cents to my name. I was in a low, dark place; for me, the simple act of brushing my teeth and taking responsibility for my own hygiene was enough to look at the next task in front of me. You may not be in that shitty of a spot. You may be complaining about a few extra pounds you added to your waistline. Maybe adding a twenty-minute walk on a daily basis would be the catalyst you need for change. Life is a series of small steps to the final destination; the hardest step is the first one.

Taking responsibility for yourself isn't an easy task. This is where your spirituality comes into play. Believing and having the willingness to lead a virtuous life can be a positive force to move you in a positive direction and potentially influence others. One small change at a time. The most difficult move is getting started. There are a lot of self-help books out there that have a lot of opinions on how to accomplish this. However, a lot of what's out there is also garbage (much like this book). No matter if you have a good book or a bad one, they all require you to take action. Take what you can use and leave the rest.

Remember that your life experience is unique to you. What may work for Mark Manson may not necessarily work for you. Use your virtues as a guiding principle and take responsibility for yourself. If you fuck up and revert back to the old behavior, give yourself some grace, forgive yourself, make adjustments, and move forward. Happiness and joy are not destinations or goals to be achieved. They are feelings that we get that are subjective and need to be treated as such. Treat moments in life, the good and the bad, as learning opportunities, and enjoy the process. To quote the Doors, "No one here gets out alive."

Chapter 10
Balancing My Life Out

Throughout this book, I've outlined some really stupid shit that I have done in my life. Some of you may have done worse, and some of you may learn from my experience and not repeat the stupidity. I didn't get this far in life by being foolish and stupid all the fuckin' time. I've written about taking responsibility and taking control of my finances. I've also mentioned that I educated myself all the way up to completing my graduate program in 2019.

So let us discuss education just for a minute. When I taught computer repair and web design between 2010 and 2013 for the Los Angeles County School District, I emphasized the importance of education. I have to stress that education doesn't have to come in the form of going to a formal university system. Most university programs offered today are garbage degrees designed to fleece you of your money and waste your time. However, if you insist on going through the university system, I highly recommend getting educated in the traditional curriculum and avoiding the humanities subjects for the most part. If you do choose the humanities route, I suggest looking into English, Philosophy, and history. I'd suggest pursuing the sciences, such as biology, chemistry, math, engineering, and computer subjects, for example (my biased opinion).

Traditional universities aren't the end-all of education. There are other options: technical and trade schools are a great resource, and at many of them, you can earn degrees like at a traditional university. However, the curriculum focuses on the trades: welding, gunsmithing, electronics, computer science— you get the point. Most tech schools have the curriculum completely laid out for you. The benefit is that all you have to do is show up and complete the requirements. I will say that these programs are intense. You will be carrying fifteen to eighteen units per semester if attending full time.

Finally, there's the military. I know what you're thinking. The military? I don't want to be in combat. Here is the thing the recruiters won't tell you: For every combatant on the front lines, there is a network of forty to seventy-five support personnel. What does this mean? Well, for every infantryman, tanker, pilot, and artillery personnel, there are personnel such as engineers, lawyers, doctors, nurses, medics, and mechanics, as well as specialists in logistics, transportation, mechanics, computers, communications, and post-hole digging (PHD). The key is to study for and score high on the Armed Services Vocational Aptitude Battery (ASVAB) Test.

In my personal experience with the army, I scored high enough on the ASVAB test to become a pilot. However, it was my own fear that kept me from being a pilot and realizing a lifelong dream. I didn't realize my potential at the age of seventeen after going to the Military Entrance Processing Station (MEPS), so I opted to be a helicopter mechanic. I remember the recruiter questioning my decision to opt out of flight school. Despite all the stupid choices I've made, this is one of my regrets. I don't have many, but not going to flight school stings, as I described in an earlier chapter. This regret was all me. I try not to dwell on it too much, human nature being what it is; I do think that maybe my trajectory could have been different and I could have avoided those DUIs early in life. My insecurities and low self-esteem changed the course of my life. I didn't believe in myself enough to take the risk, a very low risk at that.

My military experience wasn't negative in any way. Becoming a mechanic delayed my entry to flight school, but I considered it a bonus. I learned the inner workings of the machine I wanted to fly. Well, the rest is history. We know what happened afterward.

Plan B, I took advantage of the GI Bill and pursued a career in technology. I earned an Associate of Applied Science in Electronics and a Bachelor of Science in Management at a technical school, which opened the pathway to computers and cybersecurity. As a result, I also earned computer certifications from industry giants such as GIAC, Microsoft, Cisco, and CompTIA, and eventually a Master of Science in Cybersecurity. Despite myself, I've been living a comfortable life. The point is it doesn't matter where you get your education from—shit, it can be on-the-job training (OJT). What matters is that after high school, we all need a form of secondary education that is practical and useful. Lord knows, no one learns anything in the public school system anymore.

Integrity & Honesty

Fast-forward a few years, I began my consulting business. In 2002, I was self-employed. The learning curve was steep, but I managed my own business. The only people I had to answer to were my customers. I was confident in my skill set, and business was growing daily, attracting new customers via word of mouth. I was self-supporting through my own contributions. I had two cars, and at the time was renting a two-bedroom apartment in Costa Mesa, CA. Life was good.

I received a call from one of my customers I hadn't heard from in a while. I rarely heard from customers unless something was broken (meaning they had computer issues). At the time, most of my smaller customers didn't keep a maintenance plan. So most of my visits and customer base were break/ fix. I arrived on site, and the administrative assistant, Julie, my direct contact, mentioned that she couldn't retrieve some files from the server. Without getting technical and into the weeds, I began troubleshooting the issue.

Again, without getting into all the technical issues, while troubleshooting, I inadvertently deleted $27 million worth of financial records this firm was managing. HOLY SHIT! WTF? HOW THE FUCK DID I DO THAT? I was panic-stricken. I had to think fast. I accidentally deleted the hard drive from the computer system, noobie mistake 101.

Not a problem, I'll rebuild the drive and recover from backup. Until I realized that no one was changing the tapes and the information hadn't been backed up in months. *Shit, shit, shit, shit, shit* . . . Thinking on my feet, I realized that it was late on a Friday afternoon, so I calmly approached Julie and said the problem wasn't a quick fix and for her to close up shop and go home, I was going to be awhile. After Julie left, I continued shitting myself and freaking the fuck out. WTF was I going to do? Again, panic-stricken and thinking fast, I reached out for help!

By that time in my career, I had a few friends and business partners that I could call at a moment's notice, one of which was a data recovery expert, Ray. Now at this point in my career, I had some experience and understood that in order to recover data, the number one rule was, "Do not attempt to write over the disks." I shut the machine down, removed the drives, and rushed them over to Ray. I explained what had happened, and the first question he asked was, "Did you attempt to write over the disks?" Quickly, I responded, "Nope!" "Good, then it should be a clean recovery," he said.

Back in those days (in my best grandpa voice), everything was slow, well, relative to today's technology. Forty-eight grueling hours of waiting over the weekend, wondering if the data would or even could be recovered, I shit a brick the size of Catalina Island the entire weekend. Most importantly, I was trying to figure out what to say to the client—not Julie, the owner, Scott. If I couldn't get this problem fixed by Monday morning, I was royally fucked (or, to quote Turkish, "propper fucked," shout-out to *Snatch*, 2000). The potential for a lawsuit and every worst-case scenario ran through my head.

Then it happened: I got the call from Ray on Sunday night, August 13, 2006: "I got your data." I could finally breathe. Relief washed over me like water in a wet T-shirt contest, and some of the pressure was off. I picked up the data and the original drives, rushed over to the office, and began rebuilding the Redundant Array of Independent Disks (RAID) (Google it!), imported the data, and verified the client computers had access to and could retrieve the data over the network. All was good, except how was I going to save myself?

First thing Monday morning, I walked into Scott's office. I detailed everything that had transpired from Friday to late Sunday night, including the fact that I fucked up and inadvertently deleted the data. I also validated with him that all the assets he was managing were intact, including the file that was missing that spawned the original call. Finally, I didn't charge him a dime. The data recovery and the labor fees were all waived—no charge, nothing, zip, zero. I took responsibility and paid Ray for his time and materials. It wasn't cheap. Most hard lessons aren't. And I did not bother to recover those expenses from Scott.

What lesson ever is cheap? (Is there an echo in the room? WTF?) The school of hard knocks is a brutal educator. Why did I waive my expenses? Why not lie about the whole thing and invent some story? No one would know, right? I would know, and it would take my ass years to forgive myself for that type of deception. I couldn't sell out my integrity. Integrity is everything; without it, you have nothing. I could have made up some technical mumbo-jumbo and called it a day, but I couldn't do it. I'd fucked up and I owned up to it. I took responsibility and did everything I could to make reparations. I lost Scott and his business that day, and I don't blame him.

Now, I'm not perfect by any stretch of the imagination. I am human. After all, I use omission as a way of deception, which a form of lying. Not saying that deception is something to be proud of; however, this is a defensive mechanism developed at a young age, and I'm still working on it. I've just had too many instances where people (some who claimed to love me) took the words that came out of my mouth, manipulated them, and used my own words against me. Much like the assholes that will take this book out of context and use it against me. I say fuck 'em; I sleep well.

Chapter 11
Sins of a Father

The sins of the father are to be laid upon the children.

– William Shakespeare, The Merchant of Venice

Another version of this is from the Bible:

The LORD is longsuffering, and of great mercy, forgiving
iniquity and transgression, and by no means clearing the
guilty, visiting the iniquity of the fathers upon the children
unto the third and fourth generation.

—Numbers 14:18

I never read *The Merchant of Venice*, but how appropriate that
an Italian city is the backdrop in the book. I have pondered
this quote for years. There are many explanations, and of
course I have my own interpretation. My belief is that family
traits and traditions, good, bad, and indifferent, however
reasonable or unreasonable, include familial transgressions.
Children will unintentionally inherit those traits and values.
(Uncle Jesus "Sonny" Sanchez, RIP, referred to this as "genetic
continuity. He had a third-grade education, and he had the
gift of gab. He was the smartest third grader I ever met.) As
mentioned earlier, my parents were immigrants. My mother

immigrated to the United Sates from Italy in the late '50s, and my father later in the early '70s.

I was born in 1972, in Los Angeles County, making me a first-generation US citizen. So growing up was difficult in the respect that my parents had old-country (Italian) values, whereas I was growing up with a whole different value structure here in the US. Needless to say, there were many occasions where my father and I disagreed. If I were to describe my relationship with my dad, I'd say it was turbulent in the best of circumstances.

My interests were often disregarded, which meant that I had no voice under any circumstance. There were times when he would take me hunting, camping, or fishing. Where a few fond memories exist, however, those memories are overshadowed by experiences of criticism and ridicule, which affected my teenage years. In a nutshell, these experiences pushed me away from my dad. I enjoy camping, hunting, and fishing; however, I never seemed to be good enough and was constantly criticized for my performance or underperformance. As a result, I rejected hunting and fishing, regardless of how much I enjoyed the outdoor activities. There was no father-son bonding as far as I was concerned. From my perspective, these experiences always seemed to end in the negative.

The home front wasn't all that pleasant either. In the '80s, it seemed vogue to be a latchkey kid. Like most kids, when arriving home, I had chores to do. If the chores weren't completed adequately, there were severe consequences. At the time, it seemed normal; however, some of the punishments did not fit the crime.

Subsequently, in my teens, I rebelled. The rebellion took many forms: stealing cash from his wallet, sneaking out of the house after curfew, drinking alcohol, and lying (or omitting details) about all of my shenanigans. I understood clearly what the consequences would be. I built up a second life hidden from my old man. From time to time, my mom would catch me in the act. However, there were a few times when she would rat me out. If she was put in the position to spill the tea, it was because she couldn't bury the evidence of my delinquency.

To be balanced, my father would take on a second job to make ends meet. I can honestly say he never missed a day's work, regardless of his health. He provided a roof over our heads. I had clothes on my back, and to some level, he attempted to connect with me by introducing me to his hobbies. His friends loved him. He was a man's man, and he was often charitable to his friends and gave freely to them. Everything from an outsider's point of view was skewed in the positive, as opposed to my negative perspective of living with the man. It seems my dad had a double life as well.

As a young adult and in recovery, the alcoholic cloud began to lift. I tried to understand what made my father tick. We never discussed any of his experiences as a child. Honestly, I never knew my father. (I know, total cliché.) He kept his life experiences locked up tight and stuffed down. The little I did uncover was through third-party accounts, and from what I understood, he didn't have much of an upbringing himself. Actually, it was way more uncomfortable than my own experience. But does this absolve him of his sins?

Over the last thirty years, I've tried to forgive the man for being a dick. I've tried putting myself in his shoes, and in some cases, I've lived in his shoes and experienced his experiences firsthand. He made sure of it. Outsiders have asked me not to judge him harshly. He wasn't knowledgeable and didn't understand his own shortcomings. I've taken all of this into account. My conclusion is that he taught me what not to be as a human being. So I've spent the last thirty years in therapy, twelve-step programs, and reading literature on various subjects, such as religion, stoicism, and psychology, to repair my understanding of who this man was. Giuseppe died on March 24, 2021. My sister called early that morning and informed me of what had happened. Prior to his death, he and I had been estranged for eight years. The consequence, with my seeking approval, affirmation, attention, and love unrequited, I had lost all respect for Giuseppe.

In spite of his attributes, he had many character flaws that I inherited. For the most part, he rode the coattails of the women in his life. This became clear after my mother divorced him and the death of his second wife in 2015. He simply gave up on life, became nihilistic to some degree, and depended on others for support. The irony in all this is that the people that were closest to him and knew him wanted nothing to do with him. As an unfortunate consequence, my younger sister shouldered the burden of his care as his health declined. I am grateful to her and her family for the sacrifices she made.

In April of 2021, after Giuseppe's funeral, both my sister and I had to sort through his estate in Los Angeles. Sorting through the financial aspects of the estate was smooth and fair in my regard. I actually had no expectations when it came to the will. Years earlier, Giuseppe swore he had written me out of it. So why would I help my sister sort through the estate? Well because I love my sister, regardless of whatever contention had with my parents. Tanya did her best to leave the issues between me and my parents. So I naturally wanted to support her. Only God and my sister know the true sacrifices she had to make to support Giuseppe.

From April to June of 2021, I moved to Los Angeles and lived in my childhood home. While sorting through the property, the house was filthy and undermaintained. Giuseppe's garage was exactly as I described in a previous chapter, stuffed to the roof with junk and garbage. Sorting through the garage and trying to determine what was valuable versus what was junk took a huge effort. When the garage was completely emptied and cleaned—the contents of the garage had to be hauled off in three forty-yard dumpsters.

Giuseppe's garage was a metaphor for his life. He stuffed everything in it: the good, the bad, the valuable, and the shit. All the items were in disrepair and neglected, including the valuable items. And in the end, most of it was ruined and worthless. A tragic metaphor, much like his life. As if this wasn't enough, through family channels we discovered that both Tanya and I have a half-brother. Imagine discovering at forty-eight years old that you have a sibling on the other side of the planet.

While in Los Angeles, I was in therapy sessions, and many of the childhood traumas were being discussed regarding my relationship to women and my need to simp. During a video meeting with my psychiatrist, I informed her of what had transpired. She asked how I felt about Giuseppe's passing. I explained that I was relieved, as I didn't have to shoulder the burden I had placed on myself, and I no longer required his approval, affection, or attention. Giuseppe's passing represented freedom, not sadness. I felt the weight and the burden had finally been lifted.

I voluntarily took on my fathers' burdens and sins. Giuseppe ran from responsibility. And through his actions, he placed his biases, fears, hatred, and shame on me. I absorbed all of it as a child and shouldered his inadequacies through adulthood. As a consequence, I repeated his behavior, however different our life experiences were.

Chapter 12

A Boy and His Dog

In chapter 4, "Sex and Relationships," I wrote about Wife #1. (BTW, I've been married and divorced only once, so I am trying to stick to the conventions I loosely wrote about in the introduction.) In that chapter, I laid out the events of the relationship and the divorce. I also mentioned my dog, Olly. This chapter is about my dog Olly.

In my early twenties, Alcoholics Anonymous and the twelve steps laid out the foundation of how not to live like an animal. Olly was instrumental in teaching me how to be human.

In late 2016, my unit in the California State Guard was activated to support in a search-and-rescue mission in Northern California. A few days into the mission, I received a text message from Wife #1 that she had a surprise for me. I'm not a fan of surprises. (Not—I hate surprise party–level, unplanned events that are preventable or within human control.) It'd been a while, so I don't remember exactly how the conversation went (if you call texting a conversation). I guessed that she had adopted a dog. When I returned home the following weekend, we went to pick up our new family member around December 2016.

Prior to adopting Olly, my wife and I had discussed the possibility of adopting a puppy. I wasn't completely opposed to the idea. However, further discussion was required, you know, ideas like type of diet, training, outdoor vs. indoor dog, and other specifics to be discussed, so when our new family member arrived, Wife #1 and I would be on the same page. My understanding was that we would have a conversation prior to adopting a puppy. Needless to say (I'm going to spell it out anyway), we never had the discussion. We drove to the breeder in Elverta, CA, to pick up our new puppy.

Just like most Labradors, Olly was cute as pie. At first glance, he seemed completely healthy and normal around his siblings. Arriving home, we set him up in the laundry room of our 2,600-square-foot suburban home. I sat in the corner of the laundry room playing with my new pup. Wife #1 had to run out to the local pet store to gather additional supplies, and because Olly wasn't fully vaccinated, I stayed home with him. The moment Wife #1 walked out the door, I began to sob uncontrollably. Looking back and trying to understand that moment, I guess it was partly joy and partly because the responsibility involved in taking care of another soul, a living being. The idea scared me. I didn't believe that either of us was prepared.

Wife #1 flew for a major airline. She had an interesting schedule, which, very early on, I stopped trying to understand. I worked full-time in a cubicle; and the schedule was predictable and mundane. When I would go to work during the week and Wife #1 was home, she would watch Olly. The challenge was when she was out of town for a couple of weeks at a time, and I was at work between seven and five (that's right, ten-hour workdays, including commute times). Leaving Olly in his crate all day unattended did not sit well with me. However, my gracious father-in-law (at the time) would come to the house and sit and play with Olly for an hour or two around lunchtime. I was truly grateful, and his graciousness settled some of my insecurities.

I believe that Wife #1 experienced a few emotional upsets realizing that we may have bitten off more than either of us could chew. I'd like to take a second to set the stage. Wife #1 prided herself on having a clean home (almost fanatical about it). Our house was a new build in the southeast part of the Sacramento area. Like all new builds, the backyard was not completed, and minimal landscaping was in the front yard. Secondly, to this Southern California-born knucklehead, Northern California gets a lot of rain. So, you, the reader, can imagine dirt in the backyard and rain. The natural outcome was mud and lots of it. Olly, being a young pup, had to go outside to take care of business (pee and poop). He also liked to play, and he loved mud. Let's just say clean house fanaticism and a muddy puppy do not go hand in hand. Wife #1, on the verge of tears and overwhelmed, called me at work to explain her situation. Naturally, my smart ass came out and said, "We own a dog. What did you expect? You can't have a clean home twenty-four seven with a dog. That's not possible!"

Very early on, Olly and I were thick as thieves. I enjoyed playing and wrestling with the young pup. One weekend morning, while lounging on the couch, Olly propped up on my chest. I noticed he had a thousand-mile stare. For those that don't know what a thousand-mile stare is, it's when someone stares off, looking past everything, but there is no light in the eyes or focus. Many people who suffer from post-traumatic stress disorder (PTSD) display this behavior. In Olly's case, it was accompanied by a subtle head shake. I found it an odd behavior for a ten-week-old puppy. However, when I distracted Olly, he quickly snapped out of his episode, and play resumed.

Olly was a special dog. Over the next five years of his life, my then-wife and I spent a lot of time, money, and energy on Olly. There were so many veterinarian visits, and the high level of responsibility required to raise Olly was overwhelming at times. Both she and I made plenty of mistakes in his training. I don't need to get into the shit she pulled. I am going to focus on myself. As I mentioned earlier, I was working a ten-hour day commuting to and from downtown. Typically, I would arrive home around 5:45 p.m. after my commute. Olly would be sitting up on the couch, ready to greet me as I walked in the door. Immediately after my arrival home, I'd lift Olly off the couch and take him outside to go number two.

My wife and I loved the idea of snuggling on the couch with our pup. We were so excited to teach him to jump up onto the couch and share in puppy snuggles. (Yes, I said "puppy snuggles.") This is why when arriving home, Olly would be patiently waiting on the couch. One evening I had an appointment with my chiropractor, so after work, I went to my appointment and had my spine adjusted. When I arrived home, Olly was on the couch to greet me. However, there was something different in his behavior. Olly was anxious and nervous. When I approached and made my way toward Olly, I noticed a pungent smell that only increased in foulness as I got closer.

Upon closer inspection, I saw there was shit all over the couch and Olly. He'd found himself in a pickle waiting at home for Daddy to take him out, only for Dad to come home late. Poor pup defecated on the couch and, as a result, spread his feces all over himself and the couch. I picked up Olly off the couch and took him outside. Then the panic set in. What if my wife came home and I was unable to get the house clean? How would I even begin to clean up this mess? I was covered in shit.

After recovering from momentary paralysis, I saw Olly make his way back into the house via the doggy door and begin spreading his shitty footprints all over the common area of the house. Finally, I snapped out of my daze and went to the cleaning supply closet and grabbed the shitty dollar store mop. At this point, Olly's anxiety had subsided, but my anxiety began to increase. As far as Olly was concerned, Daddy was home, and it was playtime. Immediately after I reached for the mop, Olly attacked it as ferociously as a puppy could. I wrestled with Olly, and the mop disintegrated in front of my eyes . . . Noooooooooooo! I blew a gasket. I grabbed Olly by the scruff and tossed his puppy ass into his crate. At the same time, he stubbed his paw underneath the crate and hurt himself. I hurt my pup, only to add to my already shitty moment (no pun intended). I was fit to be tied. I grabbed what was left of the mop and went out into the garage and, in a fit of rage, slammed the mop handle into the floor, yelling, "FUUUUUUUUUUUUUUUUUUUK! FUCK! FUUUUUUUUUUUUUUUUK!" with every swing of the mop. Surely, my neighbors must have thought I had gone insane. There is no way in hell they didn't hear that commotion.

Once I regained my composure, naturally, I called Wife #1 to explain the situation. I was freaking out; I didn't know how to begin cleaning this mess—a very long, detailed story short. I went to the local big hardware store, purchased all the industrial cleaning supplies required to clean the mess, stripped the covers off the couch, washed them, scrubbed what couldn't be removed, and mopped the floor. When I completed cleaning, I pulled Olly out of his crate and carried him to the bathroom, and we both showered. It was a long night, a work night. I crated Olly up and passed out. The morning would come fast.

Olly and I avoided each other. He avoided me because he could sense my anger. I avoided him because I was pissed off—not at Olly, at myself. You see, the following day after work, I called my good friend Jim. He was a long-time dog owner and had a lot of experience with dogs. I explained to him in detail the events that had transpired.

Now a little history, many years ago, Jim and I bartended at the same club I mentioned earlier. Jim, a longtime friend, knew I was an asshole at times, particularly to poor tippers. He still remained my friend after all these years, regardless of how big of an asshole I could be. After my rant, he asked the question, "To what purpose did getting so pissed serve?" He went on to say, "Why are you getting pissed about poop? It's just poop!" At that moment, there couldn't have been a more profound statement: "It's just poop!"

It's just poop. It should be a metaphor for life because we, as humans, experience poop every day! That's the human condition. We experience poop. We have to navigate the poop of other humans in our life: your boss, your husband, your wife, the police, the judge, the asshole who cut you off. Poop everywhere. Of course, I thanked Jim for his wisdom. However, I still mulled over the situation that had transpired the night before for a few more days.

A few days later, the thought came to me as if God himself had delivered it. We (Wife #1) and I were so thrilled that we had taught Olly to jump on the couch, but we never taught him to jump off the couch. I unintentionally taught Olly to wait for me on the couch until I arrived home from work. I wasn't forward-thinking and hadn't taken steps to mitigate this fiasco. Much of this heartache and stress could have been eliminated if I had taken responsibility and thought his training through. In a strange way, it is a total representation of Newton's rule: "For every action, there is an equal and opposite reaction."

Olly is exactly what he is, a puppy, a dog, a K9. He doesn't have a voice that I can understand. I took on the responsibility of adopting him. As a result, Olly depended on me for his food, safety, and love. That evening shined a huge light on who I was as a human being. It's my failings that set him up for failure. And as a result, I took it out on him and Wife #1. I resented having this responsibility. Only after deep reflection did I realize I resented myself because I was ill-equipped for the responsibility.

The moral of the story is that we as humans fail on so many levels. Most of our failures are so subtle we don't recognize them, we don't realize when we practice them. We bring children into our lives under the misguided thinking that the children will improve our situation or improve who we are as members of society. We make the decision to marry, thinking that this is good for us and will strengthen the relationship.

In turn, a few short years later, we divorce. In my opinion, having children is no longer a necessity in terms of modern society.

Having children in today's world is a luxury, a luxury that we as humans are not prepared for. It's hard to ignore; the little animals we are raising (or neglecting to raise) are entitled little pricks. We allow our public school systems and/or neighborhood rats to raise them. While you are at work, achieving new levels of debt in order to keep up with the Joneses, your kids are being raised by strangers, other children, and internet porn. Then we, as parents, have the nerve to get angry at the system and deflect the responsibility to others. Look in the fuckin' mirror. Your kids are animals because you've disengaged and have no true understanding of what responsibility is.

We have multiple generations of children who are growing up with no self-respect and, as a consequence, no respect for others. Young ladies have a double-digit body count by their sophomore year in college. Young men are afraid to go outside and touch the grass. Most of them do not have the skills to read this simple-minded book written at an eighth-grade level. These are the decision-makers of our future, of your future. How is it possible that we are raising a generation of children who are incapable of leading productive lives and are lacking in discipline, integrity, temperance, and diligence? We are looking forward to very scary times. We are raising an impulsive generation that is oblivious to the consequences of their need for instant gratification.

Children, much like Olly, require copious amounts of time to train and be disciplined, to grow up, to be well-adjusted, responsible animals. Most households, if lucky enough to have two parents, may be able to take the kids to extracurricular activities. However, today's children consider a single-parent home as normal. Traditional roles have no value, and as a consequence resort to social media and the internet to whore themselves out for likes and attention. This results in them shitting all over their lives before they even have a chance to get started. Maybe we need to reconsider the shit we are putting our children through and investigate the need to bring morality back into our lives.

After my divorce, I gained custody of Olly. Two very short years later, Olly's health declined, and he was suffering seizures every few hours regardless of his medications. Early in the morning of September 10, 2021, neither of us got much sleep. Yet again, I contacted his veterinarian, a follow-up to an earlier visit that week. I took Olly to the emergency clinic that morning. I said goodbye to Olly for the last time; he didn't come home with me that day. Olly was two months short of his fifth birthday. He was my buddy, my friend, my sweet, sweet boy, and my love. He taught me to be a better, kinder, more patient, loving, and responsible human. I miss you, buddy.

Chapter 13

A Heartbeat Away from Oblivion

As I was flying over the handlebars of my bicycle, the only thought I had was, *Buddy, when I get up, I'm going to stomp on your throat, rip your head off and shit down your motherfuckin'* . . .

Luckily for the other rider and his fuckin' recumbent bike, the Old Man Upstairs had other plans. You see, after hitting the ground hard, I mean really hard, I slipped out of consciousness only to remember pictures before being laid up in ICU Wednesday, July 12, 2023, at 11:33 a.m.

That's right; I was about to wrap up this book and get ready for publishing when the Old Man Upstairs decided I needed to add another chapter.

So what happened? I was out on my daily ride, nothing out of the ordinary. At the last mile, another cyclist was on his recumbent bike, and I saw him signal to make the right turn. Being the alert cyclist I am, I adjusted to pass on his left side. Simultaneously, he decided it was a good idea to make a wide right turn, sweeping into the left lane, almost clipping my front tire. Thinking fast, I made a hard right, and at that moment, he completed his right turn, and I T-boned the recumbent cyclist. I went airborne, clearing my handlebars and his bike as well.

Images of the ambulance, emergency room, various medical machinery, and other trauma patients in the emergency room are all a jumbled-up mess of memories, not to mention my trauma doctor's eyes drew my attention. (Horny old fuck, even in the trauma station you're still looking to pick up on chicks! What is fucking wrong with you?) I'm not lucky when it comes to love; more than likely, she's married. I digress. The following day the trauma doctor came into my room and explained what had happened. She explained that I had broken eight ribs, numbers two through nine, on the right side of my body. I had an AC shoulder dislocation and a bump on my head; she used a medical term, but I can't remember what it was.

I was in the trauma section of the hospital for a couple of days, and for a minute, I began to feel sorry for myself. I asked, *Why me. Why now?* These are typical questions when one is sitting on their pity pot. As quickly as the victim mentality came, it left, and another thought came in. *Wait a minute, Why not you? It's not like you haven't experienced this shit before. You've been cycling on and off for thirty-plus years since your first DUI; it's not like you haven't broken a rib before. And it is certainly not your first time dislocating your shoulder. This isn't your first rodeo. Embrace the suck and make friends with the pain.* After breakfast, I asked the nurse if I could be disconnected from all the machines, and I rolled out of bed. This is when I lie to you, the reader, and say that I sucked up the pain and walked around the nurse's station like a boss. Nope, not at all. I sucked up the pain. I held my breath rolling out of bed because breathing was excruciating. I could only do one rotation around the nurse's station because I was so light-headed and dizzy from the pain of just walking. But I did it . . . one lap.

Breaking a rib sucks, but the good news is that the pain from breaking eight ribs is no different than from breaking one rib. Breaking one rib radiates to the other eleven; breaking eight does the exact same thing and radiates to the other four. It's fucking painful. A few days later, I was released from the ICU. It was Friday, July 14, 2023. I had strict instructions to schedule a follow-up checkup with the trauma unit to take more pictures of my ribs and lungs. I forgot to mention that my right lung also had a pneumothorax. Allow me to explain what a pneumothorax is in lay terms, because I won't be able to explain it any other way. Picture the inside of your rib cavity. There is a layer of tissue that acts like double-sided sticky tape. This tissue attaches your lungs to your rib cage and keeps your lungs fixed into position. A pneumothorax is when that sticky tape gets punctured and air seeps in between the layers, causing pressure on the lungs. (If you're a fucking doctor and your ego can't handle my explanation, then you can leave your comments at https://smpn8ez.com.)

The follow-up meeting wasn't all that great with the trauma surgeon who was there for the consultation. He wasn't happy with what was going on in my lung cavity. I guess I had internal bleeding, and fluid was building up on the right side of my chest. Now I'm no doctor, but if I had a portion of my lung collapsing because of an air bubble and the bottom half drowning in fluid, I would think my lung would collapse fully, and, well, I'd be in deep shit.

My options were to be admitted immediately, or we could "donkey dick" around (not my words, that was the professional verbiage used by the trauma surgeon) for a few weeks and see what happened. I chose to be admitted instead of the latter option. Now, I realized that I would be going into surgery, and this is where I have to say ignorance is bliss because while the surgical team seemed to be on edge, like this procedure was a big deal, I was as cool as a cucumber. No anxiety at all. Again, there is something to be said about being ignorant.

After the surgery was over, I had two tubes sticking out of my back, draining all the fluid from my chest cavity. However, the pain that I had embraced a week earlier was back with a vengeance. The nighttime nurse had to play catch-up with all the medications to finally get me to a point where I could relax, or breathe, for that matter. We are talking about all the good shit, fentanyl, morphine, and all the designer drugs (Woo-hoo!), better living through better pharmaceuticals.

Still, in the recovery room, as I was writing this chapter, I had to say I was in good spirits. Embracing the suck and enjoying the process is way easier than bitching and complaining about everything. Playing the victim doesn't work. In the past, I have played the victim and felt sorry for myself when injured, but as stated in earlier chapters, people get tired of that angle and eventually resent you, regardless of the fact that you're hurt. While I was in the hospital, during a shift change, I overheard one nurse tell another nurse that I was the easiest patient in the ward. I took it as a compliment. A few years earlier, I could have easily been the worst—miserable and unappreciative.

In times like this, you also find out who your friends are. As I mentioned, I belong to Al-Anon, and every one of my Al-Anon family group stepped up and took over the responsibility for Malcolm and Angus, my two dogs. They came to deliver food and kept the house tidy and picked up and brought the mail in. My dear friend Mark and his wife Debbi have been there for me since my divorce. They have helped me through some really shitty times in my life. Mark stepped up and carted me back and forth to doctor visits. He even cooked up a hell of a rack of ribs for dinner when I returned home from the hospital—you have to appreciate his sense of humor.

At some point in time the next week, I would have a visit with an orthopedic surgeon for my shoulder. The interesting part about this adventure was that I was still enjoying the ride. When I was not worrying about what was going on in my head and the inner noise was silenced, I could listen to what was going on around me, and I could hear other people complaining about their lots in life. I could hear nurses complaining about the shitty date they went on the night before. I could hear people complaining about the lack of service they were receiving in the ICU. I heard other people complaining about politics and their opinions regarding the state of the Union, a lot of trivial bullshit.

While all this was going on, I realized that none of it fuckin' mattered. I don't give a rat's ass about who you're fucking, I don't give a shit about politics, or world issues, I certainly don't care about global warming or whether or not your civil rights are being violated in the freest country in the world. Pssst . . . your rights aren't being violated. Just ask Brittany Griner what a Russian prison feels like.) I certainly don't give a fuck about your delusions of being a furry or whatever the fuck else you're pretending to be today. One day reality will slap you in the face, and you'll realize that you were wrong. Your opinions are wrong, your lifestyle is wrong, and all those dreams you thought of chasing are just wrong. And that's OK, because when your world comes crashing down, you'll get clarity in regard to the type of human being you are. This will be the reflection you need; you will see with crystal clarity what your life represents.

Thirty years ago, when I was stuck in my delusions and arrogance, I thought the world owed me something. What that something was, I don't know. It isn't until you get kicked in the teeth a couple of times that you realize that maybe, just maybe, your perspective on life and your thinking isn't as tolerant as you thought it was, that your contempt for hard-working, responsible people is because you were too much of a pussy to take responsibility for yourself, so you would rather have someone else make decisions for you. I understand, boo; it's hard being responsible for yourself. I also know exactly what it is to hate yourself and be uncomfortable in your own skin.

Even as I'm lying in this hospital bed, I keep going over the chain of events in my head, trying to see if I made a mistake and if I could have done something different. Sometimes shit happens, shit that is beyond our control, and when that happens, how are you going to respond? Where I'm blessed and grateful is that there are people who stepped up to the plate to help me out.

You see, in life, you'll gather a ton of acquaintances. Let me say it a different way: When shit hits the fan, you'll find out who really cares about you. There are the "friends" that will ask you if there is anything they can do for you. This is a platitude; they're really hoping that you don't ask because it'll inconvenience them. They ask and put the burden on you because, more than likely, if you are banged up pretty badly you won't even know what you need.

Then there are the friends and family who insist they must do something for you. Again, this is not for you. This is so they can feed their own ego and tell all their friends what a great human being they are because they've helped someone in need—virtue signaling at its finest. This has nothing to do with your health, your comfort, or what you need. It has everything to do with their ego and how they look from the point of view of their inner circle.

Finally is the group of friends who step up to the fuckin' plate and handle business: the neighbor who surprises you and comes picks up your keys and delivers your dog water while you're laid up, the Al-Anon family member who takes up the responsibility of feeding your dogs and making sure they are crated up at night and put outside during the day, the dear friend who, without a second thought, acts as your personal valet and takes you to your doctor's appointments, and the RN who takes the time out of her busy day to do a house call to change your bandages. And not one of these people holds resentment or expects anything in return. They just do it because they genuinely love you. They do it because they are your family.

You've heard the cliche that blood is thicker than water. Mostly narcissistic family members will use that line against you in an attempt to guilt you into thinking that the only people in life that have your best interests at heart are people with familial ties. What most people don't ever hear is the rest of the quote, "The covenant in blood is thicker than the water of the womb," meaning the people who have been through the grind with you, who have seen you bleed, sweat, and cry in agony, who have seen you at your worst and still love you, are the people that belong with you in the trenches. Those are the people that gave of themselves so that I could recover.

What's my point? I guess what I'm trying to get at, or the point I'm trying to make, is that no matter how important your delusional mind may think you are, the reality is you're not. No amount of money, power, or fame will make you a good human being. While your money will pay for comfort and you can hire good health care, it doesn't make the people you hire your friends. It's a transaction. Nothing more. If you're an asshole without money, then money will just exasperate the asshole you are. Just because you have a vagina, it doesn't absolve you of being a delusional cunt. (That's right, I said it.) Just because you're bringing down a few grand a month from thirsty simps doesn't exonerate you from being an asshole. You'll come to the reality that you've aged out and hit the wall, and you've become that crazy cat lady. (I'm just waiting for the day that pussy of yours looks like wilted lettuce.) The internet holds all your receipts. Then all I can do is laugh because you wasted your youth and your beauty for cash. And you're all alone.

I can hear all you bitches whining, "Well aren't you being judgmental?" No, no, I'm not. What I am being is discerning, choosing to keep people like you out of my life. I don't have to call you out. I don't have to cancel you or post nonsense on the internet about you. Calling you out as an asshole won't do any good; you are already well aware you're an asshole. You'll do it yourself because people will eventually come to realize that even your shit stinks (shout-out to Rob Reiner). All I have to do is walk away, stop spending money on your brands, stop watching your TV shows, and turn off the mainstream media news. It's that easy because all you are is an opinion, and a bad one at that. More about opinions a little later.

You're an overpaid rodeo clown with a delusional way of thinking. Don't worry, Hollywood, there are new outlets available for entertainment. You aren't the only game in town anymore. The only people interested in you are the suburban Karens who live in their own delusional world and are slaves to their own white guilt (dumb motherfuckers); soon enough, they'll be having their own reckoning.

I know I'm sounding a little dark right now, but the reality is if we as human beings don't stop this tribalistic mentality, then everything we find to be true will no longer exist. And we will live in some Orwellian universe. Giving up our liberties, our Constitution, and the Bill of Rights will be a huge mistake that we won't recover from.

The short of it is to be grateful, which I've mentioned in earlier chapters. It's funny how I keep coming back to gratitude. Be happy that you have a body to operate in, a body that is functioning. Become comfortable in the body you were born in. It's the only one you have. It's true your body is a temple. If you keep your temple strong, then you can survive the storms your body will go through. Secondly, reality doesn't give a fuck about your delusions. I began this chapter with a very passionate delusion of me getting up after that fall and kicking some nonplayer character's (NPC's) ass. Reality saw fit that I passed out and never got the vengeance I so delusionally believed I was entitled to. You see, reality doesn't give a fuck about your delusions.

Reality doesn't conspire for or against you, but the harder you try to deny reality, the harder your lesson will be when it comes. Give yourself a break and stop swimming upstream and ignoring reality, because there will be a huge grizzly that will swat you out of the stream and gut you . . . well, like a fish. (Where am I going with this, WTF? The oxycodone must be kicking in.) Then who do you have to blame, reality? Guess again, reality doesn't give a fuck, and neither do the millions of people who operate in reality. They don't care if your delusion wants to mutilate you and slap a meat puppet to your hip because you hate yourself. It doesn't change a thing. You're still delusional. You're still trying to ignore reality. You are still an NPC, a sideshow; that's all you'll be because you choose to live in a delusion.

I remember at thirty-eight, after moving to my home in San Diego, selling my home in La Habra, selling my car, and starting my new cubicle job, the stress level in my life maxed out and hit the red, and I got hit with shingles. The breakout happened in the lower left side of my body. Honestly, I handled that entire month like a little bitch, feeling sorry for myself and playing the victim role. The only positive I accomplished in the thirty days was I read *The Walking Dead Compendiums* one, two, and three. The blisters took over pretty much everything, including my testicles and the left side of my anus. It was a miserable experience; however, it didn't have to be in hindsight. I could have made the time a positive experience; I could have started my memoirs. I could have done anything else other than sit around and act like a little victimized bitch. It's hard looking in the mirror and realizing that victimhood doesn't work.

Start appreciating what life has to offer. Start appreciating your life. You never know when the lights will turn off and everything will be gone, when you will be in a void unable to hear anything, see anything, or feel anything—nothing but a sea of blackness, and that's it. You are one heartbeat away from oblivion. You're gone.

Chapter 14
My Experience, Strength, and Hope

The following was the speech I was supposed to give on July 22, 2023. I was supposed to share my experience, strength, and hope to an Al-Anon audience, but I never had the chance to deliver that speech because of my accident. So I'll share it with you:

> Good evening, everyone. My name is Vince. First and foremost, I'd like to thank Annette and Charlette for asking me to speak tonight. When they asked and told me I was going to be the headliner tonight, I was beside myself. *How am I going to fill thirty minutes?* Not skipping a beat, Annette assured me with my gift of gab that we'd probably run over. Hopefully, you won't be disappointed.
>
> I'd also like to lower your expectations and tell you I have no wisdom outside of the twelve steps and the literature provided to us in the program of Al-Anon. I'll share my experience, strength, and hope. And with that out of the way, let's get into this thing.
>
> #### EXPERIENCE
>
> In September of 2022, when I arrived in Al-Anon after a thirteen-year hiatus, my return differed from the usual

circumstances. I didn't have an active qualifier in my life when I arrived. I had been through a bad breakup, and it had been over a year since I had direct physical contact with her. However, with all that time that had passed, I had a hole deep down inside that couldn't be mended by any temporary fixes or distractions—no matter how hard I tried.

In the previous eighteen months, I found myself in therapy and in complete disarray, only able to manage the very basics: job and bills. Mostly, I found myself lonely and seeking attention, affirmation, and approval through less-than-desirable situations. I used people and other things to try to fill the emptiness I was feeling.

In 2021, I was barely living, much less acting and behaving like a human being. I was living in a deficit, a moral and virtuous deficit. I was merely surviving. Most of all, regret and self-loathing had begun to creep back in. I was slowly killing myself; the nihilistic thoughts and suicide began to creep into the forefront of my mind. I simply did not like the person I was becoming, the toxic person staring at me in the mirror. Most of my days were spent in a depressed state, unable to focus and confused. The ghosts of my past haunted me daily.

With God's and Al-Anon's help, I realized I needed to pull my head out of my ass. How did I get back here? What lessons do I need to re-learn? Why do I continue to attract unavailable women? I sought out professional therapy but the psychiatrist wanted to prescribe medication to help with my anxiety and depression. I responded by saying, "I already know how to sedate myself. I am goo at it. What I need is to get to the root of the issue." She insisted we poke around my childhood. I explained in a fit of frustration, "The child inside wants you to provide the adult outside with tools to get through this shit, specifically, the horrible emotions and the emptiness inside." A few weeks later, I fired her.

That's when I met my life coach and now friend, a professional business coach, Chris, who asked what I wanted to achieve from these sessions. I responded that I needed tools to help deal with these shattered emotions. My coach hailed from a similar background as mine, so he understood where I was and met me there. He provided the tools I needed to escape the pain of being involved with toxic people. However, my life still wasn't in alignment with the Old Man Upstairs, and there was something still missing—me.

I wanted to continue to sedate myself with more recklessness. Then the thought hit me: it wasn't my drinking, but my thinking. The Old Man Upstairs sends me these inspired messages occasionally, and I liken them to shock therapy. They hit me like a lightning strike, and then I change course, make the necessary adjustments, and align myself with the universe.

This epiphany led me back to Al-Anon. I had done some work in the program a few years earlier, and I returned on September 10, 2022. It took a few meetings to hear what I needed; however, the message rang loud and clear. I heard a member share his experience, strength, and hope, and much like all of you, I heard my story. I realized I was codependent and rescuing women from themselves was my modus operandi. I was the knight in lackluster armor. I needed to get a handle on this need for people-pleasing, and I needed to understand why I required people to like me. Al-Anon quickly helped me realize my issue was my relationships with others and, most importantly, my relationship with myself. I needed to find Vince again.

Most people I've encountered aren't self-reflective and typically run around oblivious to the world, selfish and concerned only about what is directly in front of their nose. This statement isn't an indictment; it is an observation.

Over the last thirty years, I have made a few observations:

My issue is that I expect too much from the general population, and I may expect too much from me. I also fear being disliked because who approves, affirms, or validates a disliked person?

I have a relationship problem with people and am addicted to anger and control. My inability to manage my reactions to people, places, and things was fostered from a young age and reinforced by impulsive behavior. I have found that the only way to correct this behavior is through the twelve steps of Al-Anon.

STRENGTH

About November of 2022, I began to work on my fourth step; steps one, two, and three were slam dunks. In my lows, I had the wherewithal to communicate with the Old Man Upstairs; he has guided me on this journey since my first DUI in 1991. I believe he has my back and never leaves me; I have conversations with him almost daily.

He allows me to be me; he accepts this vulgar child as I present myself. Steps one and two were easy to do; while on the outside, I was looking good, I could recognize my emotions were all over the board and unmanageable. I also knew that the Old Man Upstairs would guide me to where I needed to go, though typically, it requires an ass ton of hard work. He never disappoints.

This time, my fourth step was different. I am fully aware of my character defects and shortcomings—I have had the last thirty years to explore them. Or you can ask all my failed relationships; they'd happily pontificate about my shortcomings. I had to look at those positive attributes I bring to humanity and learn about Vince again. Some time ago, during my marriage, I lost who I was—and subsequently caused a horrific chain of events that led me into my own personal hell again! I had to look at my codependency issues. I had to understand why I required someone else's approval, someone outside me to validate me. I had to investigate why I placed everything I was on the back burner to accommodate someone else. I had to investigate my role when seeking attention, affection, and approval.

Before I go on, I want to provide a little more history; my father was a heavy-handed alcoholic. I spent years in other programs and therapy dealing with this truth. However, I never investigated the relationship I had with my mother. I remember an evening at a very young age when was bathed and ready for bed, and again, my mother had been the victim of my father's drunken rage. At seven I decided to save my mother, confront my dad, and give him a piece of my mind. I began to lecture him. I pleaded with him to stop drinking and told him I didn't like it when he was drunk. I said he wasn't my daddy when he drank, and I wanted him to stop hurting Mommy and to leave if he continued to treat us this way. A swift backhand to the face sent me flying across the room, and I learned four things that day:

1. How to be a hero and rescue women.

2. I didn't have a voice against authority figures.

3. How to be codependent, dysfunctional, and live in denial.

4. Anger and violence are how you shut people up.

Playing the role of martyr and victim, I learned to blame all my problems on other people (mother, father, sister, girlfriend, wife, etc.), rejecting the idea that my stupid decision put me in harm's way. My last defunct relationship with my latest qualifier perfectly exemplifies this thinking. In 2020 I purchased my ex-girlfriend's home so she could buy herself a brand-new construction in another city. Think about this for a minute: I was in love, my girlfriend needed finances, I bought her house, and she moved away and broke up with me—all counterintuitive to my plans of seeking attention, approval, and affection, much less intimacy (fuckin' genius thinking).

My fourth step helped me realize several things: I am human, and I am fallible. It taught me to accept everything about me, the good, the bad, and the ugly. It also helped me realize that I can love, not just for other people but for myself. My fifth step helped me realize that I habitually conceded, bent my knee, and moved my boundaries for many years. Every time I negotiated, accommodated someone else, and put myself last, I betrayed myself and my needs. I never learned to ask for what I needed. (Self-betrayal is a motherfucker.)

In the not-so-distant past, this realization came to a head. I was hosting a BBQ for a group of friends in my new home, the same one I had purchased from my ex. The day was going well—good food, good drink, good people, and cornhole—all the makings of a fun time. However, one of my guests suggested we move the party to a venue in Folsom to watch live music. I responded graciously, saying, "That sounds like fun. Enjoy yourselves. I'll be here when you all return." Well, guess what? You could hear the record scratch. "You're coming with us," they said. "No, I am fine where I am at," I told them. I didn't want to go. It didn't take long, and the entire party was trying to convince me to go. I didn't want to go. Yet I allowed them all to change my mind, and I went. Truthfully, I was pissed. Shortly after arriving, I left the venue abruptly, ensuring I ruined everyone else's evening because my evening was ruined. My victimhood became a weapon, and in true codependent and passive-aggressive form, I threw a grenade on the whole evening. Why? Because I had conceded and moved my boundaries.

Returning to my fourth step, I also had to recognize what a wonderful human being I am. This was the most challenging part of my fourth step. Making an honest inventory of my positive attributes is difficult for someone who suffers from low self-worth. Growing up and including my adult relationships, I could never speak of my accomplishments or positive attributes because I would be labeled a braggart, boasting, or selfish. Again, I never allowed myself to speak to my positive attributes. I never had a voice. I depended on others for affirmation and validation, but it rarely came. The accomplishments that I did achieve were rarely spoken of, and the one person I was seeking validation from died from dementia. The approval never came.

During the fourth step journey and service to Al-Anon, I realized I was compassionate, loving, gracious, knowledgeable, charitable, honest, and articulate. I am also loyal, dutiful, respectful, selfless, and honorable; I possess integrity; and I am courageous. Having to look at oneself and be honest is the most frightening thing we can do as humans. Identifying the role I played in my stupidity came naturally, being someone with low self-esteem. However, identifying what was good about me took work. I had to identify how I allowed people, places, and things to manipulate me and recognize that ignorance isn't an excuse, including evaluating my positive attributes and what is good about me. You see, I became comfortable with being an asshole because it meant I didn't have to try to be a virtuous human being. It is easier to wallow in the mud with the pigs!

Steps six and seven required me to put in additional work. Faith without work is dead. I firmly believe that statement. I had to begin to discover what it took to care for myself.

1. Be of service in the program.

2. Find what Vince likes again.

3. Become an active participant in my own life again.

In doing so, I discovered that I am loved, that I have family in the program of Al-Anon, that I love myself, and, yes, that a glass of Barbera wine with a ribeye steak is fucking amazing. I've also learned my limitations: I am learning to speak up when particular requests don't work for me. I avoid spreading myself thin. I can say no without getting angry. I also realize that when someone is gaslighting me, I can choose not to participate. Sometimes no response is the most powerful response.

Steps eight and nine helped me to forgive myself for doing so much damage to my life. I forgave myself for neglecting myself, for allowing my fears to run my life, and for allowing horrible humans to dictate how I should live. Step ten is my checks and balances; when I am operating in fear or become angry, I can pause and ask myself, "Why did that sting?"

Step eleven has been the backbone of my recovery for many years. I remember a quick anecdote about this concept in early 2018, conversing with the Old Man Upstairs. Things were not going well in the marriage, there was no communication, and the marriage had devolved into a sexless one; we were utterly indifferent to each other, completely devoid of love. I was on my way to work, in the car alone—this is where the Old Man and I have our best conversations. I recall asking him should we (my then wife and I) get a divorce. Two weeks later, he answered: she announced she wanted a divorce. My smart ass replied, "Don't let the door hit you where the good lord split ya!" (Progress, not perfection.) The concept of step eleven reminds me that it's my responsibility to seek out his wisdom and maintain the connection; when

I neglect to seek out his council, I drift from his grace to my detriment.

Step twelve, if tonight doesn't prove that step twelve is working, I don't know what to say.

Between steps four and ten, the singular most important tradition in my life was tradition seven: "Every group ought to be self-supporting, declining outside contributions." My most glaring issue is my inability to trust the Old Man Upstairs. After years of being prey to gaslighting by people in my life whom I thought loved me and had my best interest at heart, I made the mistake of trusting these people, relying on them to make my decisions for me, and thinking their opinions mattered more than mine or the Old Man's. The seventh tradition helps me remember that I have to be able to stand on my own two feet. It began slowly, taking care of my financial house and ensuring that I was fiscally responsible. With this concept in mind, I began to operate more freely regarding financial concerns. Paying bills was no longer an issue—the literal interpretation of the seventh tradition.

Then I realized the spiritual premise behind tradition seven and how it related to people outside of me. Returning to what I said earlier, I allowed outside contributors to sway me in important life decisions. The example of buying a house comes to mind. At that time, somewhere in the back of my mind, in my heart of hearts, I knew I was making a mistake, ignoring my instincts to affirm someone else's idea to gain someone else's approval, affection, and attention. Tradition seven is a stopgap to prevent me from being persuaded by outside influences. Easier said than done, step seven proves that when I trust my instincts, prepare and educate myself, and trust the Old Man Upstairs, life seems smoother, juxtaposed to being held accountable to someone else financially or emotionally.

Tradition seven reminds me to be a pillar, to stand on my own. It also reminds me to contribute to my spiritual recovery bank. I am taking the actions required for those days when I have to withdraw from my seventh tradition account.

On July 12, 2023, I had to make a huge withdrawal from my account. I was involved in a cycling collision traveling at speeds of up to twenty miles per hour. I went over the front handlebars of my bike and over the other cyclist who was involved. The first thing that went through my head was, as soon as I get up from this fall, I am going to shove my foot down your fuckin' throat. Luckily for him, God had different plans; not much is remembered after I went unconscious.

In the emergency room, as I was drifting in and out of consciousness, the doctors and nurses were asking me to provide emergency information and contacts. However, both my emergency contacts live in Idaho, my primary a permanent resident, and my secondary a part-time resident, only to return in two days. My emergency contact told the ER case worker about Malcolm & Angus, my two seven-month-old puppies. The caseworker then asked who could take care of the dogs, and I asked her to contact Judy, a fellow member of my Friday night group (the same group that is hosting tonight). In a drug-induced one-handed text, I sent a signal flare to my group:

"Hey, Judy, will be getting a call from hospital I was admitted to. Long story, but I'll need some help with the boys."

If I could compare the response to any one thing, it would be like the flight of the Valkyrie scene in *Apocalypse Now*. The Old Man Upstairs had sent the fuckin' cavalry! Within seconds the entire group lit up the thread and coordinated to help me and my pups. This reinforced the idea that Jim shared with me in a meeting that Al-Anon is my family.

The following morning in ICU, the attending emergency room doctor came to visit during her rounds. She informed me that I had a separated shoulder, eight total broken ribs on the right side of my body (ribs 2-9), acute pneumothorax, where the lining separating my chest cavity and lungs was punctured, multiple contusions and abrasions, and a bump on my noggin, so no real damage to my head.

As I was lying there in ICU, I did have a moment of "Why me?" and a pity party. However, as quickly as the thought came, it passed. It was replaced with, "Why not you? Embrace the suck and enjoy the journey." Gratitude seeped in, and I realized I was alive, that my body, regardless of the damage, was strong. I called the nurse to help me disconnect from the machines. I wanted to take a few laps around the nurse's station. I'm not Superman, so the fuckin' pain was excruciating. But the worst part was over; the self-doubt and self-pity came and went. The seventh tradition reinforces the concept that I am a pillar; I am strong with the Old Man Upstairs and my Al-Anon family group.

I rely on specific steps more than others; this is where I am in my recovery. However, there is no mistaking the spiritual, philosophical, and psychological impact of the twelve (12) steps. Each step is weighted slightly differently, depending on where I am in my recovery. Still, there is no mistaking that the twelve (12) steps and twelve (12) traditions are of divine inspiration, created by some very learned men and brave and courageous women.

HOPE

I want to remain open and teachable. I want to continue discovering who Vince is and peel back more layers of debris. I plan to continue to learn about philosophy and stoicism. I hope to be the virtuous good man I am meant to be. There is a caveat to hope: it is contingent upon action. Every time I buy a lottery ticket, I can hope for a million dollars. However, it seems ironic to be hoping for something based on a short cut, all the while financially taxing myself when buying that "winning" ticket. Hope requires work, diligence, and perseverance; hope requires working toward a virtuous life.

To live a virtuous life, I must remember to give grace and not react with judgment. I need to afford myself that same grace and respond with kindness. It's a true statement that how I treat myself is how I would treat people. In other words, I treat people as I would treat myself. What this means to me and how I behaved in the not-so-distant past is, the same contempt I held for myself was the contempt I secretly held toward other people. I remind myself daily to let go of the contempt and be gracious and patient with myself and others.

Happiness and joy aren't goals to be achieved like a college degree. Hope, happiness, and joy are found in the processes of life. The mundane duties and tasks that are required of me in life are there to teach me lessons daily, enjoying putting one foot in front of the other. What a concept, to enjoy the simple ability to walk, both physically and metaphorically. I do not take anything in life for granted, most of all who I am and the good I can bring to the world. I plan to continue to meet more positive people like the ones I've met in this program.

Before my accident, I had the most remarkable day a few weeks ago. I started the day early and joined a group of friends for pickleball. It didn't matter who won or lost—just the ability to enjoy the day with friends and meet new friends that morning. Later, I enjoyed bathing both my dogs in their brand-new bathtub. Malcolm & Angus didn't enjoy the process nearly as much as I did. I went on an eleven mile ride around Lake Natoma, scouting out new trails and the possibility for adventure and, finally finished out the day at a Brazilian-style BBQ restaurant where I met the general manager and the great staff, all while enjoying a fantastic dinner. I need to remember days like these to get me through the challenging ones. I must remember to be grateful to the Old Man Upstairs who has never left my side; I also have to be thankful to him for introducing the twelve steps to me all those years ago. Because of the twelve steps, I am learning to be virtuous human and a good man.

Today if you were to ask me if I am cured of my codependency or adolescent behavior, I would snicker; it would be like asking me if I am cured of my humanity. These character defects are ingrained into my psyche and the fibers of my being. A better question would be how I manage my compulsive behavior; I would then respond with the following.

1. God, first and foremost.

2. The Twelve Steps.

3. These behaviors do not serve me today.

4. Finally, mind my own fuckin' business.

My character defects are two sides of the same coin, whether self-medicated or sober—fear, anger, and contempt are miserable feelings to live with. I am the common denominator, and it is my choice what I do and whom I choose to associate with—unlike when I was a child and had no voice and much less choice. As an adult, I need to develop my ability to make wise choices. And in recognizing this, I am accountable and responsible for the misery I allow people, places, and things to bring into my life. I have a voice.

I'd like to close with something from Mark Twain:

> Life is short; break the rules, forgive quickly, kiss slowly, love truly, laugh uncontrollably, and never regret anything that makes you smile.

> Thank you for your time and consideration and for allowing me to share my story. Luv ya, mean it!

Chapter 15
Conclusion

Finally, this book is over; I'm sure that every page was used wisely and flushed down the toilet after wiping your ass. In that regard, much like all self-help books, action is the key. Like my buddy Jim who called me out on my bullshit, refused to cosign my self-pity, and refused to acknowledge my victimhood stated, only you can change you, and only you can change your circumstances in life.

I set out to write a self-help book, and I have accomplished that very thing. In writing this Pulitzer Prize-winning novel, I helped myself. It's been four months since my last cigarette. I've adopted two new puppies, Malcolm and Angus. I've lost another ten pounds and broken the two hundred-pound threshold, I now weigh one hundred ninety-eight pounds, which means I've lost a total of sixty pounds since my divorce. I have a brand-new truck in the garage; yes, that's right, I can fit a mid-size truck in my garage, and still have room to store tools and bikes. I am learning to be single and rebuilding my frame. And shortly, this book will be edited and published. If you're reading this, I've met my goal.

Most of this self-help book is subjective based on my own personal experiences. Your experiences in life will be different. And just like most self-help books, subjective material is bullshit, and some of it is accurate and relevant. Take what you can use and flush the rest down the toilet. However, if there is one point that I would recommend paying attention to, it is to take responsibility for your life. Fuck everyone else's perception of you and do you.

Become comfortable in your skin, and don't let outside influences fuck with you and your potential. Find people who are a net positive in your life and who have moral values that align with your own and learn from them. Personal virtue is nonnegotiable; deep down inside, you recognize when you are in self-betrayal and people-pleasing. Finding yourself in toxic relationships and conceding to the whims of others, being foolish and stupid, and simping just doesn't work.

Remember to be flexible and open, realize that nothing is in stone or concrete. Points of view and perception change as new information and circumstances change. Give yourself grace if you fuck up, realign and adjust, make room for the new information learned and move forward. Failure isn't a setback; it is an opportunity to learn new skills. "Improvise, adapt, and overcome," is one of the army's mottos that has served me well over the years, even in some of the stupidest situations I've found myself in. Never forget, the Old Man Upstairs has your back. Be open to him, and soon enough you'll be having conversations with him, and he will respond. (You may not like some of his answers, so be careful of what you ask for!)

Be leery of the bullshit on the Internet. People will pretend to take a moral high ground; in reality, they are virtue signaling. Typically, these people are morally corrupt themselves. Don't take what you see on social media too seriously; these people are getting paid to make you feel like shit, investigate the audience base and find out where these influencers make their money. Most of the time, like our politicians, they are getting paid large sums of money or kickbacks to pander to special interests.

For those of you I have offended, I have a little something I'd like to share with you from one of the best punk bands during my teenage years"

Just 'cause you don't understand what's going on

Don't mean it don't make no sense

And just 'cause you don't like it, don't mean it ain't no good

And let me tell you something

Before you go taking a walk in my world

You better take a look at the real world

'Cause this ain't no Mister Roger's Neighborhood

Can you say, "Feel like shit"?

Yeah, maybe sometimes I do feel like shit

I ain't happy 'bout it, but I'd rather feel like shit than be full of shit

And if I offended you, oh, I'm sorry, but maybe you need to be offended

But here's my apology and one more thing, FUCK YOU!

—Suicidal Tendencies

I can't relay the importance of abstaining from the internet. Stop giving away to influencers—Hollywood, reality TV stars, social media, local news channels or athletes—the one asset away we can never get back: time. These people are entertainers, glorified clowns. They stand for no other purpose than to make a buck. Your time is finite and much too valuable to be wasted on the bullshit these jokers are peddling!

One last thing, and probably the most important advice I received in life:

Opinions are like assholes. Everyone has one, and they all stink!

Bonus Chapter
Technology Is a Wonderful Thing?

During the course of this writing, OpenAI made public ChatGPT. To summarize, ChatGPT is an artificial intelligence platform that basically is smarter than you, or me, for that matter. So in toying with the technology, I had ChatGPT draft a twelve-step program for simping. It was modeled after the twelve steps of Alcoholics Anonymous, a program that has helped millions of humans all over the world get control of their addictions. Who knows? This could go somewhere, or it could fall flat. Either way, spiritual principles are powerful tools that can help you out of that hole you dug yourself into.

SIMPING RECOVERY

Step 1

The first step toward recovery is admitting that one has a problem with simping and that it is causing problems in their lives. This concept can also be applied to broken relationships. Admitting that there is a problem in the relationship and taking responsibility for one's actions is the first step toward healing and moving forward.

When a relationship ends, it is easy to place blame on the other person and refuse to take responsibility for one's own actions and emotions. However, true healing and growth can only come from taking an honest look at oneself and acknowledging one's role in the relationship's demise. This can be a difficult and painful process, but it is an essential part of moving on and finding happiness.

When a relationship ends, it can be a very emotional and stressful time. People often experience a wide range of feelings, such as sadness, anger, and hurt. During this time, it can be easy to place blame on the other person for the problems in the relationship or to see oneself as the victim. This type of thinking can be comforting in the short term, as it allows individuals to avoid taking responsibility for their actions and emotions. However, it is not a constructive approach to healing and can ultimately prevent one from moving on and finding happiness.

True healing and growth can only come from taking an honest look at oneself and acknowledging one's role in the relationship's demise. This means being honest with oneself about one's actions, emotions, and behaviors and how they contributed to the problems in the relationship. It also involves taking responsibility for one's mistakes and understanding that you are not a passive victim in the relationship's demise.

This process can be difficult and painful, as it requires one to confront difficult truths about oneself. It is easier to avoid this process, or to try blaming the other person for everything, but true healing can only come from acknowledging one's role in the relationship and taking responsibility for one's actions. It's also important to note that it's not always one person's fault that the relationship ended. It could be the result of different circumstances, issues, and incompatibilities in the couple.

This acknowledgement not only allows one to learn from their mistakes and grow as a person, but also helps to ease feelings of guilt, shame, or resentment toward the other person, which can be barriers to move on. By taking ownership of one's role in the relationship, individuals can begin the process of moving forward and finding happiness.

One should find happiness in the process of healing, not just as an end goal. Engaging in self-reflection and introspection, seeking therapy or counseling, and focusing on personal growth can bring a sense of purpose and fulfillment during what can be a difficult and lonely time. It can also help one to become a better and more self-aware partner in future relationships.

Personal growth is an essential aspect of life that can bring a sense of purpose and fulfillment during difficult and lonely times. The process of personal growth involves taking stock of oneself, identifying areas for improvement and working toward becoming the best version of oneself. Through this process, individuals can gain a sense of direction and purpose in their lives, which can be especially important during challenging times.

One of the main benefits of focusing on personal growth is that it can provide individuals with a sense of agency and control in their lives. When faced with difficult and lonely times, it can make one feel as though one has no control over their circumstances. However, by focusing on personal growth, individuals can take control of their own lives and work toward becoming the person they want to be. This can be empowering and can help to mitigate feelings of helplessness and hopelessness.

Additionally, personal growth can lead to the development of new skills and abilities. When individuals work toward becoming the best versions of themselves, they may find that they have the opportunity to learn new things and take on new challenges. This can be extremely fulfilling and can provide individuals with a sense of purpose and direction. Furthermore, new skills and abilities can open up new opportunities and possibilities, which can help to mitigate feelings of loneliness and isolation.

Personal growth can also lead to the development of deeper and more meaningful relationships. As individuals work toward becoming the best versions of themselves, they may find that they are better able to connect with others. They may also find that they are more authentic and truer to themselves, which can lead to more meaningful and satisfying relationships.

Additionally, it's important to understand that in some cases, a relationship may be toxic or destructive with no happiness within it. It is important to understand that not all relationships are healthy or positive. In some cases, a relationship may be toxic or destructive, and true happiness within it may not be possible. These relationships can cause emotional and mental harm, and it may be necessary to end the relationship in order to ensure one's well-being and happiness.

A toxic or destructive relationship can take many forms. It may come in the form of verbal or physical abuse, manipulation, or a lack of mutual respect and trust. In such a relationship, one may be constantly walking on eggshells or may feel constantly demeaned or belittled. These feelings can result in a lack of self-worth and self-esteem and can negatively impact mental health.

Furthermore, a toxic relationship may also affect one's physical well-being. Chronic stress, which can come from being in a toxic relationship, is linked to a host of physical health issues, such as heart disease and diabetes.

In some cases, individuals may try to make the relationship work by making excuses for the other person's behavior or downplaying the negative aspects of the relationship.

It is important to note that leaving a toxic relationship can be difficult, especially if one has feelings for the other person or if the relationship has been long term. However, it is important to remember that in toxic or destructive relationships, the well-being and happiness of an individual are most important. It may be helpful to reach out for support from friends, family, or professionals such as therapists to help navigate this process.

In conclusion, acknowledging one's role in a broken relationship and taking responsibility for one's actions is the first step toward healing. Finding happiness in the process of personal growth and self-reflection can bring purpose and fulfillment during a difficult time. It is crucial for both parties to take responsibility to understand the part they played and to learn and grow from the experience to build a better future relationship.

STEP 2

Step two states, "Came to believe that a Power greater than ourselves could restore us to sanity." This step is crucial in the recovery process for individuals struggling with simping, and it can also be applied to relationships and sex.

In the context of relationships and sex, step two encourages individuals to believe in something greater than themselves that can help them overcome their addiction. This may involve belief in a higher power, such as a deity or the universe, or it may involve belief in a community of support, such as twelve-step groups or therapy. By placing faith in something greater than oneself, individuals may find the strength and guidance they need to overcome their addiction and make positive changes in their lives.

Step two also relates to the idea of surrendering control. This is the idea that the individual can't control everything, specially concerning their addiction. By admitting that they are powerless over their addiction and turning to a higher power for guidance, individuals can let go of their need to control every aspect of their lives and instead trust in something greater than themselves. This can bring a sense of peace and relief and can help individuals to focus on their recovery and growth.

In the context of relationships, step two can help individuals understand that they cannot control the actions or behaviors of others, but they can control how they respond to those actions and behaviors. By surrendering control to a higher power, they can find the strength to let go of toxic relationships or unhealthy patterns in their relationships.

Step two of simping recovery can be particularly useful for individuals struggling with sexual addiction because it helps them understand the power of addiction and how it can impact their sexual behavior. Understanding the power of addiction can help individuals recognize that they are not in control of their addiction and that they cannot overcome it on their own. This realization can be difficult, but it is also the first step toward recovery.

Simping or sexual addiction can manifest in a variety of ways, such as compulsive masturbation, excessive use of pornography, or engaging in risky or promiscuous sexual behavior. These behaviors can be difficult to control and can cause a range of negative consequences, such as relationship problems, financial difficulties, and damage to one's mental and physical health.

Step two of simping recovery can provide guidance on how to let go of unhealthy sexual behaviors. By admitting that they are powerless over their addiction and turning to a higher power for guidance, individuals can find the strength and support they need to let go of these behaviors. This can involve setting boundaries, seeking therapy, and finding healthy outlets for sexual expression.

In addition to providing guidance on how to let go of unhealthy sexual behaviors, step two of simping recovery can also help individuals seek help for sexual addiction. By recognizing that they cannot overcome their addiction on their own, individuals may be more likely to reach out for help and support. This can involve joining a support group, such as Sex Addicts Anonymous (SAA), or working with a therapist who specializes in addiction and sexual behavior.

In summary, step two of simping recovery can be particularly useful for individuals struggling with sexual addiction. It can help them understand the power of addiction and how it can impact their sexual behavior. It provides guidance on how to let go of unhealthy sexual behaviors and how to seek help for sexual addiction. It may involve a process of admitting powerlessness and seeking support from a higher power, therapy, or support groups such as a twelve-step program. It's important to notice that seeking help and support is essential in the recovery process from sexual addiction.

Step 3

Step three of simping recovery states, "Made a decision to turn our will and our lives over to the care of God as we understood Him." This step is an important part of the recovery process for individuals struggling with addiction, and it can also be applied to relationships.

In the context of relationships, step three encourages individuals to make the decision to turn their will and their lives over to a higher power, which can be understood as God, a higher power, or a community of support, such as a twelve-step group.

Step three of simping recovery can be particularly difficult for individuals who have been in control of their relationships or have had difficulty trusting others. This is because the step requires individuals to let go of their own control and trust in something greater than themselves. For those who have been in control of their relationships, letting go of control can be a difficult and uncomfortable process. They may be used to being in charge and making decisions, and the idea of turning their will and lives over to a higher power can be daunting.

Additionally, for those who have had difficulty trusting others, the idea of trusting a higher power can be challenging. They may have been hurt or betrayed in the past, and the idea of placing their trust in something or someone else can be unsettling. They may be skeptical of the idea of a higher power and may question whether it is even possible to trust something they cannot see or touch.

Furthermore, for those who have been in control of their relationships, they may have difficulty trusting others because they believe no one can take care of them as well as they can. They may have difficulty delegating responsibilities and may feel uncomfortable relying on others for support. This mindset can make it challenging for them to turn their will and their lives over to a higher power, as they may not feel comfortable relying on something or someone else for guidance and support.

In spite of these difficulties, it's important to remember that step three is a process and does not require immediate perfection. It's a willingness to take a step toward a different direction. It's also important to keep in mind that the step is not about giving up control or trusting blindly. It's about recognizing the limitations of self-will, and seeking guidance and support from a higher power, to assist in the process of recovery.

Codependency refers to a type of relationship in which one person enables another person's addiction, poor mental health, immaturity, irresponsibility, or underachievement. In a codependent relationship, the codependent person may feel responsible for the other person's behavior and well-being and may put the other person's needs before their own. In order to overcome codependency and establish healthy relationships, individuals in recovery must learn to trust in themselves and others and to set healthy boundaries.

Letting go of the need to control others or to be controlled is also an important aspect of step three. This can be difficult for people in recovery, as addiction and other issues often stem from a need to control one's environment and emotions. Learning to respect the boundaries of others and setting your own is crucial for achieving and maintaining healthy relationships and for becoming self-sufficient and independent. This step requires trusting in the process and making a decision to follow the guidance of a higher power, whatever that may be, to overcome the harmful patterns and reach the road of healing.

Step three also relates to the idea of humility. By humbly admitting that they are powerless over their addiction, individuals can begin to let go of their ego and need to be in control. This can be a crucial step in the process of healing relationships, as humility allows individuals to admit mistakes and seek forgiveness. This step can be important for rebuilding trust in relationships and learning to forgive and to be forgiven.

Letting go of the ego and the need to be in control is a central aspect of many personal growth and self-improvement practices. The ego is the part of the self concerned with one's own image and identity. It is often driven by the need for validation, power, and control.

When individuals let go of their ego and their need to be in control, they can begin to see things from a different perspective and become more open to different ways of thinking and being. They become more accepting of themselves and others and less reactive to the judgments, opinions, and expectations of others.

In the context of recovery, letting go of the ego and the need to be in control can help individuals let go of the past behaviors, patterns, and habits that led to their addiction or other issue. It allows them to acknowledge their own powerlessness and look for guidance and support, to find a new purpose and values to live by.

It can also help them to let go of the negative self-talk and judgments they may have been holding onto and replace them with self-compassion and self-acceptance. This can be a difficult process, as the ego can be deeply ingrained in one's sense of self, but with time and practice, it can be done. Finding a support group, going to therapy, or working with a therapist can be useful for working on this.

In addition, step three helps individuals to understand that they are not alone in their struggles. By turning their will and their lives over to a higher power, they can find the support they need to overcome their addiction and build healthier relationships. They can also find a community of support that can help them heal and grow.

In conclusion, step three of simping recovery is an important step in the recovery process for individuals struggling with simping, and it can also be applied to relationships. This step encourages individuals to make a decision to turn their will and lives over to a higher power, which can provide them with the strength and guidance they need to overcome simping and make positive changes in their relationships. It also relates to the idea of humility, letting go of control and understanding you are not alone in your struggles. This step can be crucial for rebuilding trust, healing, and growing.

Step 4

Step four of simping recovery, also known as the "moral inventory," is a process in which individuals take a deep and honest look at themselves and their past behaviors. This step is a crucial part of the recovery process, as it allows individuals to gain insight into the patterns and behaviors that led to their addiction and take responsibility for their actions. We will discuss how the principles of step four can be applied to the context of broken relationships.

One of the key components of step four is self-reflection. In order to take a moral inventory, individuals must be willing to examine their past actions and behaviors with a critical eye. This means facing the truth about their mistakes and taking responsibility for them. In the context of broken relationships or simping, this can be a difficult and painful process. It may require individuals to confront past hurt and betrayal and acknowledge the ways their actions may have contributed to the breakdown of the relationship.

However, by taking a moral inventory and taking responsibility for their actions, individuals can begin to understand the underlying patterns and behaviors that led to their relationship problems. This self-awareness can help them to avoid repeating the same mistakes in future relationships. It can also help them learn how to communicate effectively, set healthy boundaries, and develop empathy. By working through their past relationship issues, they can also learn how to work on their own self-growth and emotional healing.

Another important aspect of step four is the idea of making amends. In the context of broken relationships, this may mean reaching out to the person with whom the relationship wa broken and apologizing for any wrongs committed. This can be a difficult and uncomfortable process, but it can be an important step in the healing process for both parties involved.

It's important to note that making amends does not necessarily mean expecting the other person to forgive or reconcile. It's a gesture of remorse that helps us heal and move on. It is also important to respect the other person's boundaries, feelings, and choices. Furthermore, making amends can also mean a willingness to forgive the other person for any wrongs that were committed. Holding onto grudges and resentment can prevent individuals from moving forward and healing from their past relationship issues.

Low self-esteem and self-worth are prevalent issues that can have a significant impact on an individual's overall well-being. Self-esteem is the value or worth an individual assigns to themselves, while self-worth is the belief in one's own inherent value as a person. When an individual's self-esteem and self-worth are low, it can lead to a number of negative consequences, such as depression, anxiety, and a lack of self-confidence. In this essay, we will explore the causes and effects of low self-esteem and self-worth, as well as ways in which individuals can improve their self-esteem and self-worth.

One of the main causes of low self-esteem and self-worth is negative self-talk. Negative self-talk is the habit of speaking to oneself in a negative or critical manner. This can include thoughts such as "I'm not good enough" or "I'm a failure." Negative self-talk can be triggered by experiences such as childhood trauma, bullying, or negative feedback from others. When an individual is constantly exposed to negative self-talk, it can lead to a lack of self-confidence and low self-esteem.

Another cause of low self-esteem and self-worth is social comparison. Social comparison is the act of comparing oneself to others. When an individual constantly compares themselves to others, it can lead to feelings of inadequacy and a lack of self-worth. This is particularly prevalent in today's society, where social media and other forms of technology make it easy to compare oneself to others and to be exposed to a curated, idealized version of reality.

Low self-esteem and self-worth can also be caused by unrealistic expectations. When an individual sets unrealistic expectation for themselves, they are more likely to feel like they are not measuring up to those standards. This can lead to feelings of failure and inadequacy, which can further contribute to low self-esteem and self-worth.

Low self-esteem and self-worth can have a number of negative effects on an individual's life. They can lead to a lack of self-confidence, which can make it difficult for individuals to take risks and try new things. They can also lead to a lack of motivation, as individuals may not believe in their own abilities. Low self-esteem and self-worth can also lead to social isolation, as individuals may not feel comfortable around others or may not feel like they have anything to contribute. In addition, low self-esteem and self-worth can have a negative impact on mental health, increasing the risk of depression, anxiety, and other mental health issues.

To improve one's self-esteem and self-worth, it is important to work on changing negative thought patterns and behaviors. One effective way to do this is through cognitive-behavioral therapy (CBT), which can help individuals identify negative thought patterns and replace them with more positive ones.

Practicing self-compassion and self-forgiveness can also be beneficial. It is important to practice empathy and to remember that everyone makes mistakes and has flaws. This can help to increase self-worth and build self-compassion.

Another effective way to improve self-esteem and self-worth is through self-care practices. This can include activities such as exercise, relaxation techniques, and spending time in nature. It also includes getting enough sleep, eating well, and taking care of your physical well-being. Engaging in activities that bring joy and pleasure can also help boost self-esteem and self-worth.

Step four of Simping Recovery Anonymous, also known as the *moral inventory*, is applicable to the context of low self-esteem and low self-worth. The process of taking a moral inventory involves examining one's past behaviors and actions and taking responsibility for them. This process can be particularly beneficial for individuals struggling with low self-esteem and low self-worth, as it can help them gain insight into the patterns and behaviors that have contributed to their feelings of inadequacy and self-doubt.

One of the key components of step four is self-reflection. This means examining one's past actions and behaviors with a critical eye and taking responsibility for any mistakes made. In the context of low self-esteem and low self-worth, this can involve facing past experiences such as childhood trauma, bullying, or negative feedback from others, which may have contributed to negative self-talk and negative thought patterns. By taking a moral inventory and taking responsibility for one's actions, an individual can begin to understand the underlying causes of their low self-esteem and low self-worth, which can help them work through these issues and improve their self-esteem and self-worth.

Another important aspect of step four is the idea of making amends. In the context of low self-esteem and low self-worth, making amends may involve apologizing to oneself for past mistakes and forgiving oneself for any wrongs that have been committed. This can be an important step in the healing process, as it helps individuals let go of past hurt and resentment and develop self-compassion. Furthermore, it can also include setting realistic expectations for oneself and learning to see oneself as worthy and valuable, regardless of past mistakes.

The concept of setting realistic expectations for oneself and learning to see oneself as worthy and valuable, regardless of past mistakes, is an important aspect of building self-esteem and self-worth. When individuals set unrealistic expectations for themselves, they are more likely to feel like they are not measuring up, which can lead to feelings of failure and inadequacy. Setting realistic expectations for oneself means being honest with oneself about one's abilities and limitations and setting goals that are achievable.

It also means understanding that everyone makes mistakes and that failure and mistakes are a normal part of life. Instead of seeing mistakes as evidence of one's unworthiness, it's important to learn from them and grow from them. Recognizing that everyone makes mistakes and that we are all human can help reduce feelings of shame and self-doubt.

Learning to see oneself as worthy and valuable, regardless of past mistakes, can be a difficult process, but it's crucial for building self-esteem and self-worth. It's important to recognize that self-worth is not something that can be earned or controlled, but it's an inherent quality of each individual. Every person is worthy and valuable, simply by being alive. This can be hard to believe when we're struggling with self-esteem issues, but developing self-compassion and empathy can be helpful. It's also important to work on changing negative thoughts and behaviors and to surround oneself with positive and supportive people.

An effective way to develop self-worth, self-esteem, and self-compassion is to practice gratitude. Being thankful for the blessings, big or small, in our lives and focusing on them instead of dwelling on our mistakes can shift our focus from negative thoughts and judgments to positive emotions and actions. Additionally, engaging in activities that bring pleasure, joy, and accomplishment can help develop a sense of self-worth and good feelings about oneself.

In conclusion, setting realistic expectations for oneself and learning to see oneself as worthy and valuable regardless of past mistakes is a crucial aspect of building self-esteem and self-worth. It's important to understand that we all make mistakes but that these mistakes don't define and are an opportunity to learn and grow. By practicing self-compassion, empathy, gratitude, and positive activities, individuals can learn to see themselves as worthy and valuable regardless of their past mistakes and create a new narrative of self-worth and self-esteem.

Step 5

Step five of simping recovery is the "admission of wrongs" step, in which individuals admit to God, themselves, and another human being the exact nature of their wrongs. In the context of relationships and self-worth, step five can be a powerful tool for healing and growth. In this essay, we will explore how the principles of step five can be applied to the context of relationships and self-worth.

One of the main benefits of step five is that it allows individuals to take responsibility for their actions and behavior. In the context of relationships, this means admitting to any past mistakes or wrongs that have been committed and taking responsibility for them. This can be a difficult and uncomfortable process, but it can also be incredibly liberating. By admitting to past mistakes and taking responsibility for them, individuals can begin to understand the patterns and behaviors that have led to the breakdown of their relationships. This self-awareness can help them avoid repeating the same mistakes in future relationships and develop healthier patterns of communication and behavior.

Another benefit of step five is that it allows individuals to express their remorse and remorseful actions. It's important to remember that this step is not meant to be an attack on someone else, but to take responsibility for one's actions and express regret for any harm that may have been caused. Apologizing and making amends can help individuals let go of past hurt and resentment and begin to heal their relationships. It also allows one to develop empathy and understanding toward others.

Apologizing and making amends is a key aspect of step five and can be particularly beneficial when it comes to letting go of past hurt and resentment in relationships. When individuals apologize and make amends, they are acknowledging the harm they have caused and taking responsibility for the actions. This can be a powerful tool for healing, as it allows individuals to express remorse and seek forgiveness.

Apologizing and making amends can also help break down barriers and open up lines of communication, which is essential for healing and rebuilding relationships. It allows both parties to express their feelings, thoughts, and perspectives and to work toward understanding and forgiveness. This can be a difficult and uncomfortable process, but it is an important step toward moving on and healing the relationship.

Making amends can also include actions that repair the harm caused, and it can take many forms, such as reparations, acts of kindness, or simply expressing remorse and regret. It's important to note that the goal of making amends is not to change the past, but to take responsibility for one's actions and seek forgiveness and redemption.

Furthermore, the act of apologizing and making amends can be beneficial for an individual's self-growth and emotional healing. It allows individuals to let go of past hurt and resentment and focus on forgiveness, empathy, and understanding. It can also lead to an increase in self-worth and self-esteem as individuals begin to understand the impact of their actions on others and take steps toward making things right.

Additionally, step five is an opportunity to practice vulnerability, to share one's innermost thoughts, feelings, and fears with another human being. It's a step that requires trust and courage, and it can also be a step that leads to self-discovery, a deeper understanding of oneself, and a sense of liberation. When individuals share their stories, they can connect with others, and gain perspective and understanding, especially when it comes to understanding their own mistakes and how they affect others. This can help to improve self-worth and self-esteem.

From a philosophical perspective, the opportunity to practice the vulnerability that step five of Simping Recovery Anonymous presents is rooted in the idea of authenticity. *Authenticity* is the concept of being true to oneself and living in accordance with one's own values and beliefs. Practicing vulnerability involves being open and honest about one's thoughts, feelings, and fears, which requires a level of self-awareness and self-acceptance. When individuals practice vulnerability, they are able to be authentic and true to themselves.

Authenticity also involves letting go of the need to be perfect or conform to societal expectations. When individuals practice vulnerability, they are able to let go of the need to present a perfect image to others and to be honest about their flaws and weaknesses. This can be a difficult process, but it can lead to a deeper understanding of oneself and a greater sense of self-acceptance.

Furthermore, vulnerability is often associated with the concept of vulnerability as strength, in which vulnerability is seen as a sign of courage and strength rather than weakness. Being vulnerable means to reveal one's innermost thoughts and feelings, which can be a difficult and uncomfortable process, but it can also be a powerful tool for building connections with others and fostering empathy and understanding. When individuals are able to be vulnerable and share their stories, they open themselves up to connecting with others.

In conclusion, apologizing and making amends can be a powerful tool for letting go of past hurt and resentment in relationships. By acknowledging the harm that has been caused and taking responsibility for one's actions, individuals can open up lines of communication and begin to heal their relationships. Additionally, it's an act of self-growth and emotional healing, as it allows individuals to focus on forgiveness, empathy, and understanding. It can also lead to an increase in self-worth and self-esteem as individuals begin to understand the impact of their actions on others and take steps toward making things right.

Step 6

Step six of simping recovery, also known as the "readiness to have God remove these defects of character," can be applied to the context of low self-esteem, self-worth, and relationships. The principles of step six can be used to address these issues and to improve overall well-being.

One of the main benefits of step six is that it allows individuals to identify and confront the negative patterns and behaviors that have contributed to their low self-esteem, self-worth, and relationship issues. This step requires a deep level of self-reflection and honesty, as individuals must be willing to admit to their shortcomings and to take responsibility for their actions. By identifying these negative patterns and behaviors, individuals can begin to understand the underlying causes of their problems, which is a crucial step in the healing and change process.

Another benefit of step six is that it allows individuals to ask for help and guidance in addressing these issues. This step involves asking God or a higher power to remove these defects of character, which can be seen as a symbol of humility and willingness to change. It also means to be open to guidance, wisdom, and inspiration from others, such as friends, therapists, family members or other members of the simping recovery community. This can be a powerful tool for individuals, as it allows them to access a higher level of wisdom and understanding than they might be able to access on their own.

Step six also allows individuals to practice humility and let go of the need to control everything. By admitting to their short-comings and asking for help, individuals can learn to let go of the need to control everything and to trust in a higher power. This can lead to a greater sense of inner peace and self-acceptance, which can improve self-esteem and self-worth.

Low self-esteem and self-worth can often be rooted in a deep-seated need to control and a fear of failure. This is because when individuals feel they do not have control over their lives or circumstances, they may feel inadequate or worthless. Additionally, when individuals are afraid of failure, they may be less likely to take risks or try new things, which can also lead to feelings of inadequacy and low self-worth.

The need to control and the fear of failure can manifest in a variety of ways. For example, individuals with low self-esteem may have a hard time delegating tasks or may struggle with the idea of others taking charge. They may also have a hard time accepting feedback or criticism and may feel defensive when others make suggestions or try to help them. On the other hand, fear of failure may manifest as perfectionism, procrastination, or avoidance of certain activities or responsibilities altogether.

Finally, step six enables individuals to take action toward change by being willing to take actions that align with their values and principles and put into practice what they've learned in the previous steps. This step is not just about acknowledging the negative patterns but is about taking actions to change them, through continued self-reflection, self-improvement, and self-care.

In conclusion, step six of Simping Recovery Anonymous can be a powerful tool for addressing low self-esteem, low self-worth, and relationship issues. By identifying and confronting negative patterns and behaviors, asking for help and guidance, practicing humility, and taking action, individuals can improve their overall well-being, grow and heal from their experiences, and develop a sense of self-acceptance and inner peace.

Step 7

Step seven of simping recovery, also known as "humbly asked Him to remove our shortcomings," can be applied to the context of relationships and self-worth. In this step, we will explore principles that can be used to improve relationships and increase self-worth.

One of the main benefits of step seven is that it allows individuals to take responsibility for their actions and to ask for help in changing their behavior. In the context of relationships, this means acknowledging any negative patterns or behaviors that have contributed to relationship issues and humbly asking for help in changing them. This step requires humility and a willingness to admit one's own shortcomings and take responsibility for one's actions. This can be a difficult and uncomfortable process, but it can also be incredibly liberating, as it allows individuals to take control of their behavior and make positive changes in their relationships.

Another benefit of step seven is that it allows individuals to practice self-compassion and forgiveness. Asking God or a higher power to remove our shortcomings means accepting that we are not perfect, that we are human, and that we make mistakes. As individuals practice self-compassion and forgiveness, they can learn to let go of past hurt and resentment and to focus on forgiveness, empathy, and understanding. This can lead to an increase in self-worth and self-esteem as individuals begin to understand the impact of their actions on others and take steps toward making changes.

Another benefit of step seven is that it allows individuals to let go of their ego and their need to control everything. Low self-worth and self-esteem can often be rooted in a need to control and a fear of failure. By asking for help and guidance, individuals can learn to let go of their need to control everything, and to trust in a higher power. This can lead to a greater sense of inner peace and self-acceptance which can improve self-worth and self-esteem.

Step seven also allows individuals to practice humility and ask for forgiveness. Humility is an important aspect of this step, as individuals must be willing to admit their mistakes

Step 8

Step eight of simping recovery, also known as "made a list of all persons we had harmed and became willing to make amends to them all," can be applied to the context of relationships and self-worth. In this step, we will explore the principles that can be used to address these issues and improve overall well-being.

One of the main benefits of step eight is that it allows individuals to take responsibility for their past actions and make amends to those they have harmed. This step requires a deep level of self-reflection and honesty, as individuals must be willing to admit to their past mistakes and take responsibility for the harm they have caused. By making amends and taking responsibility for their actions, individuals can begin to heal relationships and improve their self-worth and self-esteem.

Step eight also allows individuals to practice humility and empathy. By taking the time to make a list of all the people they have harmed and actively working to make amends, individuals are able to understand the impact of their actions on others. This can help foster empathy and understanding and can also help individuals to let go of past hurt and resentment. Additionally, by making amends and working to improve relationships, individuals can learn to trust and build deeper connections with others.

Additionally, step eight requires a willingness to make amends, which means being willing to take action toward change. It also means being willing to accept the consequences of one's actions, whether it be accepting rejection or forgiveness. This step is about taking responsibility for one's actions and making an effort to repair the harm caused.

Finally, step eight is an opportunity to practice forgiveness, not just toward oneself but also toward others. Making amends and seeking forgiveness can be a powerful tool for letting go of past hurt and resentment, and it can help individuals improve their self-worth and self-esteem by letting go of guilt and shame.

In conclusion, step eight of Simping Recovery Anonymous can be a powerful tool for addressing relationships and self-worth issues. By taking responsibility for past actions, making amends, and practicing humility, empathy, willingness, and forgiveness, individuals can begin to heal relationships, improve their self-worth and self-esteem, and develop deeper connections with others. It's an ongoing process of self-reflection and self-improvement that can lead to a deeper understanding of oneself and a sense of peace and liberation.

Step 9

Step nine of simping recovery, also known as "made direct amends to such people wherever possible, except when to do so would injure them or others," can be applied to the context of relationships and self-worth. In this essay, we will explore how the principles of step nine can be used to address these issues and improve overall well-being.

One of the main benefits of step nine is that it allows individuals to take action toward making amends for the harm they have caused. This step requires a deep level of humility and willingness, as individuals must be willing to admit to their past mistakes, take responsibility for their actions, and actively work to make things right. By making direct amends, individuals can begin to heal relationships, improve their self-worth and self-esteem, and build deeper connections with others.

Another benefit of step nine is that it allow individuals to practice empathy and understanding. By making amends, individuals are able to understand the impact of their actions on others and to take responsibility for the harm they have caused. This can help to foster empathy and understanding, and it can also help individuals let go of past hurt and resentment. Additionally, by making amends, individuals can learn to trust and to build deeper connections with others.

It's important to note that step nine doesn't mean to force amends. It also implies respecting others' boundaries and freewill. If someone doesn't want to receive amends or if it would harm them or others, it's important to respect that and find another way to make amends, such as expressing remorse, making amends through actions, or making amends through prayers.

Step nine also allows individuals to practice forgiveness, not just toward themselves but also toward others. It's a step that requires humility, empathy, understanding, and a willingness to let go of past hurt and resentment. It allows individuals to let go of guilt and shame and to improve their self-worth and self-esteem.

In conclusion, step nine of simping recovery can be a powerful tool for addressing relationships and self-worth issues. By taking action toward making amends, practicing empathy, understanding, forgiveness and respecting boundaries, individuals can begin to heal relationships, improve their self-worth and self-esteem, and develop deeper connections with others. It's a step that requires humility, willingness, empathy, and understanding, and it can lead to a deeper sense of inner peace, self-acceptance, and liberation.

Step 10

Step ten of simping recovery, also known as "continued to take personal inventory and when we were wrong promptly admitted it," can be applied to the context of relationships and self-worth. In this step we will explore principles that can be used to address these issues and improve overall well-being.

One of the main benefits of step ten is that it allows individuals to continuously reflect on their behavior and take responsibility for their actions. This step requires ongoing self-reflection and honesty, as individuals must be willing to admit when they are wrong and take responsibility for their actions. By continuously taking personal inventory, individuals can identify negative patterns and behaviors that may be harmful to themselves or others and take steps to change them.

Another benefit of step ten is that it allow individuals to practice humility, accountability, and integrity. By promptly admitting when they are wrong, individuals are able to take responsibility for their actions and make amends when necessary. This can help foster trust and deeper connections in relationships, as well as improve self-worth and self-esteem.

Step ten also allows individuals to practice self-awareness, self-improvement, and self-care. By continuously taking personal inventory, individuals are able to identify areas of their life that may be in need of improvement, whether it be physical, emotional, mental, or spiritual. This can help individuals grow and become the best versions of themselves.

Finally, step ten allow individuals to practice forgiveness, not just toward oneself but also toward others. It's a step that requires humility, self-awareness, self-improvement, and self-care and allows individuals to let go of guilt and shame and improve their self-worth and self-esteem.

In conclusion, step ten of Simping Recovery Anonymous can be a powerful tool for addressing relationships and self-worth issues. By continuously taking personal inventory, practicing humility, accountability, integrity, self-awareness, self-improvement, and self-care, individuals can identify negative patterns and behaviors that may be harmful to themselves or others and take steps to change them. This can help improve relationships, foster trust and deeper connections, and improve self-worth and self-esteem. Additionally, by promptly admitting when they are wrong, individuals can practice humility and integrity and take responsibility for their actions. By practicing forgiveness and self-awareness, individuals can let go of guilt and shame and improve their self-worth and self-esteem. Overall, step ten is an ongoing process of self-reflection, self-improvement, and self-care that can lead to a deeper sense of inner peace, self-acceptance, and liberation.

Step 11

Step eleven of simping recovery, also known as "sought through prayer and meditation to improve our conscious contact with God as we understood Him, praying only for knowledge of His will for us and the power to carry that out," can be applied to the context of relationships and self-worth. In this step, we will explore the principles that can be used to address these issues and improve overall well-being.

One of the main benefits of step eleven is that it allows individuals to connect with a higher power for guidance and support. This step involves seeking a deeper understanding of one's relationship with God or a higher power and asking for the knowledge of His will for us and the power to carry it out. By connecting with a higher power, individuals can gain a sense of inner peace, self-acceptance, and guidance that can help them improve their relationships and self-worth.

Another benefit of step eleven is that it allows individuals to practice humility and surrender. By seeking knowledge of God's will for us, individuals are acknowledging that they are not in control and that they need guidance and support. This can help individuals let go of their ego and their need to control everything, and it can lead to a greater sense of inner peace and self-acceptance.

Step eleven also allows individuals to practice mindfulness and self-awareness through meditation. By practicing meditation, individuals are able to quiet their minds, focus on the present moment, and gain a deeper understanding of themselves, their thoughts, and their emotions. This can help individuals identify negative patterns and behaviors that may be harmful to themselves or others and take steps to change them.

Finally, step eleven allows individuals to practice gratitude and humility. By seeking to improve conscious contact with God, individuals are expressing gratitude for the guidance, support, and blessings in their lives. Additionally, by seeking knowledge of God's will for us, individuals are acknowledging that they don't have all the answers and that they need guidance and support. This can lead to a sense of humility and surrender, which can improve self-worth and self-esteem.

Step 12

Step twelve of simping recovery, also known as "having had a spiritual awakening as the result of these steps, we tried to carry this message to simps and practice these principles in all our affairs," can be applied to the context of relationships and self-worth. Step twelve can be used to address these issues and improve overall well-being.

One of the main benefits of step twelve is that it allows individuals to share their experiences and strength with others. By carrying the message of recovery to other simps, individuals can help others to achieve the same level of healing and growth they have experienced. This can be a powerful way to improve relationships and self-worth, as it allows individuals to give back and make a positive impact on the lives of others.

Another benefit of step twelve is that it allows individuals to practice the principles of the program in all areas of their lives. By practicing the principles of the program in all areas of their lives, individuals can achieve a greater level of balance and well-being, which can improve relationships and self-worth.

Step twelve also allows individuals to continue their spiritual growth and development. By working with others and carrying the message of recovery, individuals can continue to deepen their understanding of themselves and their relationship with a higher power. This can lead to a greater sense of inner peace and self-acceptance, and it can help individuals improve their relationships and self-worth.

Finally, step twelve allows individuals to practice service and altruism. By carrying the message of recovery to others, individuals are expressing a willingness to serve and help others, which can improve self-worth and self-esteem. Additionally, by practicing the principles of the program in all areas of their life, individuals can become more compassionate and empathetic, which can improve their relationships and self-worth.

In conclusion, step twelve of Simping Recovery Anonymous can be a powerful tool for addressing relationships and self-worth issues. By sharing experiences and strength with others, practicing the principles of the program in all areas of their life, continuing spiritual growth and development, and practicing service and altruism, individuals can improve their relationships, self-worth, and self-esteem. It's a step that requires humility, service, spiritual growth, and altruism, which can lead to a deeper sense of inner peace, self-acceptance, and liberation.

Acknowledgments

Cover Design—Antonio Cesar

First Editor—Michelle Morgan

Recommended Reading

Extreme Ownership	Jocko Willink and Leif Babin
Can't Hurt Me	David Goggins
Unfuck Yourself	Gary John Bishop
The Tactical Guide to Women	Shawn T Smith, PsyD
Men on Strike	Helen Smith PhD
Stoicism—Live a Life of Virtue	Ryan James
How to Think Like a Roman Emperor	Donald Robertson
No More Mr. Nice Guy	Dr. Robert a Glover
The Subtle Art of Not Giving a Fuck	Mark Manson
The Warrior Book of Virtues	Nick Benus, USMC et. al
The Book of Numbers	Aaron Clarey
Sex at Dawn	Christopher Ryan and Cacilda Jetha
The Rational Male	Rollo Tomassi
The Unplugged Alpha	Richard Cooper
No Ego	Cy Wakeman
It's All Your Fault	Bill Eddy, LCSW, Esq.
12 Rules for Life	Dr. Jordan B. Peterson
The Naked Communist	W. Cleon Skousen
Iron John	Robert Bly
The Courage to Be Disliked	Ichiro Kishimi, Fumitake Koga
Stoicism: The Art of Happiness	Brian Sandler
Nation of Victims	Vivek Ramaswamy
Communist Manifesto	Friedrich Engels, Karl Marx
Rich Dad Poor Dad	Robert Kiyosaki
The Total Money Make Over	Dave Ramsey
I Will Teach You to Be Rich	Ramit Sethi

YouTube Channels of Interest

Better Bachelor

Jordon B. Peterson

The Rubin Report

California Insider

Mark Manson

Entrepreneurs in Cars

Katt Williams

The Rational Male

Megyn Kelly

The Ramsey Show

Man Talk

Russell Brand

John Stossel

Candace Owens

Black Conservative Perspective

Triggernometry

Kim Iverson

TimCastIRL

JRE—Joe Rogan Experience

Matt Walsh

Self-Publishing
School

NOW IT'S YOUR TURN

Discover the EXACT 3-step blueprint you need to become a bestselling author in as little as 3 months.

Self-Publishing School helped me, and now I want them to help you with this FREE resource to begin outlining your book!

Even if you're busy, bad at writing, or don't know where to start, you CAN write a bestseller and build your best life.

With tools and experience across a variety of niches and professions, Self-Publishing School is the <u>only</u> resource you need to take your book to the finish line!

DON'T WAIT

Say "YES" to becoming a bestseller:

https://self-publishingschool.com/friend/

Follow the steps on the page to get a FREE resource to get started on your book and unlock a discount to get started with Self-Publishing School.

ABOUT THE AUTHOR

Vincent Gervasi wore many hats in his life: son, brother, soldier, student, employee, employer, consultant, uncle, and husband. The bedrock on which all of his life's success has been built is taking ownership of his life and taking responsibility for his successes as well as his failures.

Vincent currently lives in a comfortable home in Northern California with his two Labrador dogs. Many of his passions include psychology, philosophy, and the human condition.

To contact the author and receive updates, feel free to visit https://smpn8ez.com.

Can You Help?

Thank You for Reading My Book!

I really appreciate all of your feedback, and I love hearing what you have to say.

I need your input to make the next version of this book and my future books better.

Please leave me an honest review on Amazon letting me know what you thought of the book

Thanks so much!

Vincent Gervasi

Made in the USA
Las Vegas, NV
07 March 2024

86867195R00114